- LIVE RICHLY!

Matt Ham

Praise for Redefine Rich

"*What is it to live a rich life, full of true wealth, and satisfying in all ways? Matt Ham has packed this book with all the wisdom you need in order to answer that question, and attain that elusive quarry—a good life blessed with the most precious riches of all. Join him on an adventure that you'll immensely enjoy, and from which you'll greatly benefit!*"

—Tom Morris
Author of *True Success*

"*Richness isn't about net worth, in the same way as wealth isn't about income. Matt Ham's book tells the story of how he came to understand that living richly comes from your heart, from relationships, from things that last. Figure that out, and your life can be truly rich despite its hard parts, which Matt knows well. Redefine Rich is inspiring, heartwarming, and powerful.*"

—W. Lee Warren, MD,
Author of *No Place to Hide:
A Brain Surgeon's Long
Journey Home from
the Iraq War*

"'Rich' is way overused in contemporary culture. In his new book, Matt Ham takes us back to the ancient and authentic sense of rich—the richness of life in joy, sorrow, complex challenges, and simple pleasures. Through the eyes of people who have faced true richness and drawn attention to its source, he shares stories and insights we should all remember on a daily basis. Yes, this book is for the business person seeking richness but also for the human soul. Great reminders that will, simply put, remind you to live a more true and robust life. And in the process, collect the richness all around you."

—Celia Sheneman
Principal/Founder,
The Maris Group

"Matt Ham sets out to redefine rich, and he does just that. He presents a clear picture of richness that collides with what rich seems to be. The stories provide clarity and the practical steps provide hope."

—Mike Ashcraft,
Senior Pastor at Port
City Community Church
and Co-Author of
My One Word

redefine
RICH
A New Perspective
on the Good Life

Matt Ham

www.redefinerich.com
www.mattham.com

Published by LIFEᵑ Media Holdings, LLC

Copyright ©2015 by Matt Ham.
Published 2014.
ISBN: 978-0-9792374-4-7
First Printing.
Printed in the United States of America.

For more information:

LIFEᵑ Media Holdings, LLC
Jim Van Eerden, Chief Editor
13 Magnalia Forest
Stokesdale, North Carolina 27357

Foreword

Sometimes a story is given to the most unlikely people—men or women (even children) who were not formally trained in the craft of storytelling, but who are given something that simply must be shared with the world.

Matt Ham has been entrusted with *Redefine Rich* in this way.

When LIFE° Media had the privilege of helping publish and promote a little book called *The Ultimate Gift,* I remember feeling the same way. That book went on to sell more than 5 million copies worldwide and became an award-winning film. It impacted the way that people thought about true wealth and the ways that they can pass on an inheritance of values to those in the generations trailing them.

As ancient wisdom reminds us, there is nothing (really)

new under the sun. From time immemorial, the pursuit of riches has animated the human experience. The challenge in any good dialogue about The Big Questions—like the question of how we become rich—is to begin by defining our terms in an accurate and helpful way.

Matt does that, and more, in this journey through stories that remind me of a favorite quote from C. S. Lewis:

> In reading great literature I become a thousand men and yet remain myself...I see with a myriad of eyes, but it is still I who see...I transcend myself; and am never more myself than when I do.[1]

Reading *Redefine Rich* reminded me that I am a rich man in ways that are not measured in financial statements. It also gives me inspiration, as it will you, about how to live richer still. And for that, I'm grateful to Matt, and grateful that we have the privilege of bringing you this important little book about the life well lived.

Jim Van Eerden

LIFE[n] Media

Magnalia Forest, North Carolina

Contents

To Liz, SHMILY
To Matthew, Wyatt, and Greyson,
may you leave a rich legacy
To my family, for always being there

Introduction

Here you are, holding this book in your hands. Whether you chose it yourself or received it from another, I'm grateful you've arrived at this moment, this exploration of richness. And as you'll read, you'll learn that I don't take circumstance lightly. Rather, I believe in purpose. And I believe this book holds a purpose for you.

Now, if you've taken the initiative to open the cover and begin reading the words on the pages, I'm honored. I hope you'll find the contents helpful—at the very least, enjoyable.

I wrote this book in response to a nudge—an unmistakable whisper I couldn't shake from my mind as much as I tried. As a husband, a father, and a small business owner, I had plenty to occupy the hours of my days. Quite honestly, I had never written before, but when this voice grew into an unavoidable calling, I felt compelled to respond.

This book, like many others I suppose, has been a labor of obedience—a labor of love. I've spent many prayerful mornings poring over the words, attempting to properly convey the story that has been laid upon my heart, my life. What you'll read is the culmination of this story up until now. However, I do believe with all I am that this story is not over.

As you turn to the pages within, I ask that you'd think with me on two possible conclusions:

The first conclusion: You are not rich by any stretch of the imagination. However, there is a curiosity about richness that you lean toward. Whether it's material items or a more stable financial future, you see richness as an aspiration. That's good. I believe that's a starting point. I ask that you open your mind to the possibility that there is much more to being rich than simply your wealth, or desired wealth. I suspect you may already know that, but you're not sure how to explain it. My hope is that this book would provide you a way to contextualize your longing for richness to include a much deeper, well-rounded pursuit of what I call true riches.

On the other hand, you may not be rich and have no desire to become rich. You're perfectly content with your financial state. That is wonderful! Actually, congratulations are in order. True contentment is one of the most difficult virtues to understand and achieve. However, just entertain with me the idea that your contentment is rooted somewhere within this deeper meaning of *rich*. This book, then, will give you the ability to define and engage in a rich life, employing the stories and principles to better tell your own story and enrich your own legacy.

The second conclusion: You are rich. Finances are not a problem or point of contention for you. However, despite your financial well-being, you're unfulfilled. The riches you experience leave you empty. The finest wines and fastest cars leave you longing for finer wines and faster cars. Within that chase, you ask yourself, "Is this it?" Regardless of your view of the afterlife, at some point, you realize that you will die. What then will become of your riches? Is there more to being rich than what you've come to understand?

Along this same line, perhaps you are rich and you do understand a diverse wealth of personal and material blessings. Moreover, you use those blessings to the benefit of others. I believe this book will magnify your view of true riches and enable you to continue your stewardship of a rich life.

As a child growing up on the East Coast, I often went to the beach to play in the surf and dig in the sand. At the time, I didn't pay attention to anything beyond the gratification and enjoyment of the moment. I was content, and the experience was both memorable and complete. Now, as an adult, I've come to appreciate not only the physical environment, but the deeper parts of the surroundings as well. The vastness of the ocean and the countless grains of sand create the atmosphere that engulfs my senses. This level of appreciation affords me the same pleasure of swimming in the surf and playing in the sand, but also the depth and maturity of the greater picture in which I am participating.

Certainly some of you may be forever content to simply enjoy the external factors and never gaze into the vast expanse of the ocean, reveling in its majesty. There is a certain level of enjoyment at hand, but it is a far cry from the fullness available to us.

The same is true of richness. I understand that many people may only want to pursue the physical gratification of riches, but I encourage you to open yourself to the fullness that awaits you upon a more profound search.

As you begin reading, I invite you to stand on the shoreline and gaze at the broad horizon before you. I promise it won't take away from your experience at all. It will only make it richer.

Richly,

Matt Ham

Part One
The Story of Richness

CHAPTER 1

A Story Waiting to Be Told

Hospital lighting gives off a unique glow. It's not particularly comforting or welcoming. On this day, its presence reminded me that I wasn't in control.

I held tight to Liz's hand, the only thing I knew to do. I just wanted her to know I was there with her and for her. The pressure from her grip and the anguish on her face reflected the pain shooting through her body. She had been like this for over two hours, and she was exhausted. While her drain was both physical and emotional, mine was purely emotional. For someone who was usually calm and collected, I was completely out of my element; there was nothing I could do. I rubbed ice chips over her lips, listening intently, and praying to hear that one sound we'd waited to hear for so long: the cry of our newborn son.

The indescribable joy when that tiny scream finally came overwhelmed us both.

This joy soon turned to fear when the doctor quickly discovered that our son's umbilical cord was tied in what they refer to as a "true knot". Inside of his mother's womb, my son had configured his only sustaining lifeline into a knot, essentially cutting him off from that which would give him life. In rare cases, this can cause developmental issues in newborns, so we waited as the doctors ran initial response tests to make sure everything was okay. Those minutes seemed to last forever.

In hindsight, this danger is oddly similar to my perception of my own journey. Tying a knot in my lifeline, suffocating myself from true life. In many cases, this event was not intentional, but my further wrestling for freedom on my own terms often tied the knot tighter and tighter.

In the case of our baby boy, we were nervous, but Liz and I had learned to rest in the truth: the One who was in control. We were here and we had faith that He would bring us through.

The doctors finally handed us our son, telling us that everything was fine. We sat there holding our baby and cried, all three of us together. In that moment, the three years of infertility faded away. The financial concerns disappeared. A marriage on the brink of destruction came back to life.

We had a son, Matthew Derrick Ham, Jr.

Eight months later, we learned that not only was God redeeming, but He has a wonderful sense of humor. We were expecting identical twin boys. In November 2011, we welcomed Wyatt Douglas and Greyson Boyd into our family.

Three boys in fewer than two short years. It was surreal. We found ourselves raising our sons and building our dream home in Wilmington, North Carolina. We embraced our faith and we loved our church, Port City Community, where we had great friends.

Somewhere in the middle of these experiences, I discovered a new connection with God. And this connection led me to a deeper understanding of the surface-level faith I had previously practiced. A heart-level change had taken place within me; I could tell this was the type of change I needed to grow.

Even so, I have to admit it was in this period that I started feeling a stirring in my soul, a dissatisfaction that I couldn't explain. It wasn't coveting—the kind of dissatisfaction that reflected selfishness and greed. This was different—much different. For months, I swatted the feeling away like I would a mosquito buzzing around my head. Much as I tried, though, I couldn't escape it.

In time, I began to recognize this stirring as a directive to tell this story. But who would care to listen to it? I was only thirty-one, and though I'd surely struggled in my post-college years, the stories truly worth telling, I thought, were about near-death experiences or overcoming great odds to build an empire or living through tragedy. The stories that deserved an audience were told by someone else. Business leaders. Thought leaders. Innovators. Needle movers. Difference makers.

I wasn't any of those.

I was a husband, a father, and an insurance agent. Responsibility had long since quieted the ambitions of my youth. However, I couldn't hush this still, soft voice within.

I want you to write.

Having no idea what I would say or what I would even consider writing about, I continually silenced these whispers. There's an element of fear that comes along with even talking about these inner thoughts because, quite frankly, determining their source is an odd quandary. It's often that internal motives rule the theater of the mind. Or is it something else? I figured I should talk about it with someone whom I knew had been there.

Within a week's time, I was having lunch with this friend despite his demanding schedule. Years before, this friend had left a tenured position at the University of Notre Dame to pursue a career in speaking and writing. Over the prior twenty-five years, he had published twenty-one books and was an in-demand resource to corporations looking to him for wisdom.

We shared very intentional conversations throughout this process. During our initial meeting, I told him about the thoughts that were feverishly racing through my mind with the concern that followed:

What would I possibly write about?

His answer changed everything.

Just grab a pen; it will come to you.

Before I could begin really writing with purpose, I grabbed my old journal, the one constant element throughout my post-high school career. The pages were scattered over the years, but as I read, I began to see that this wasn't just banter from old memories. Rather, these were my defining moments. As I read, I began to see that they were a necessary part of my journey. I took time to see the story that was unfolding within my own life. A story I had been blind to while living within it.

I sat at my kitchen table, filled with raw emotion as I revisited these tales from my journal. Victory. Defeat. Joy. Sadness. Pleasure. Pain. These were my stories, and they were pointing me somewhere.

I searched for a common theme, something to bring me wisdom regardless of the outcome. With a desire to help others and add value to someone's life, I started writing what I had learned—the good, the bad, the ugly, and the really ugly. Thoughts and emotions flooded the page. I wasn't sure which were coming faster, the words or the tears. I felt I was being turned around and given the gift of clarity as I relived my past in my mind; some stories as insignificant as mild comments, some being the milestone moments in my life. Each one taught me something incredibly important and meaningful.

In this moment, I wasn't approaching my past, or life itself, with regret. My life's experiences were all necessary because they brought me exactly where I'm supposed to be. I read back through what I'd put down, and a single word appeared in my head, even though it wasn't on any of the pages I'd written.

Rich.

It had been a road-sign word throughout my life. I had chased richness before and watched it crumble. And there were times when I realized my pursuit of material possessions wasn't the source of my joy. Rather, in those moments, I was pursuing another type of richness. Deeper—more complex.

Like a mission trip to the Bahamas, where I played the guitar for boys and girls who lived in the poorest conditions imaginable, yet they taught me of a richness beyond the comfort of any bed.

There was the day I said *I do* to the love of my life. And the night I fell to the floor in tears as I heard the cry of my first son, in awe that the family I'd long dreamed of building with my wife was now right in front of me.

And there were the four weeks of sitting in the Neonatal Intensive Care Unit with my twins as they learned how to use their lungs. As I held them to my chest and sang, richness radiated through my veins.

It was through these moments I realized being rich had far more to do with my heart than it did my wallet.

Up to this point, it seemed that I lived my life in reaction to a world I didn't understand. A world seemingly shrouded in negativity. The term *good news* didn't seem to exist. Everywhere I turned, there was another tragedy, and I'd question. There were glimpses, or beacons of light, on occasion that touched my soul and brought me hope. But with the changing of the seasons, my life tended to slip back into a routine.

I felt an internal draw to richness; however I now know it was often the world's definition—one rooted solely in financial prowess.

What some might call, the good life.

In this mind-set, life seemed to be a constant comparison. Stronger. Better. Richer. Smarter. Happier. Culturally, I felt trapped. Chained by some invisible force. Tied down in bondage to a system of ideals and principles I didn't understand. Vacations didn't last long enough, my children were growing up too fast, and someone else always seemed to have it better.

I would tell myself, *if you just work harder, keep up, run the race, play the game, get ahead, you'll eventually get there.* As I awaited this arrival, expectations began to grow. Like a three-year old from the backseat, I'd question, "Are we there yet?" This pursuit of richness lured me along the path, pressure mounting with every step to keep up. Truthfully, the good life didn't seem so good after all.

Is this really it? I wondered.

And in that moment, I identified what was to be the next step of my journey. For years I had been trying to define richness in one form or another. Now, I felt the charge to redefine my pursuit and then share it as a way to help others combat the challenges and struggles of their own.

Observations

The pain of our circumstances often drowns our flame, doesn't it? A constant routine of hope and struggle drains the very joy from our souls.

It seems as if we are living between the beacons—trying to make it until we see the glimmer of hope as the next one emerges on the horizon. When the distance between those beacons becomes too long for us, we seek more in much variety. We try to fabricate this light in our lives, longing to grab hold of that flame of hope. Quite simply, we consume. That consumption, while temporarily freeing, costs. It costs us our energy, our commitment, and our money. In the end, we trouble and toil, only to feel consumed and broken.

Maybe there are glimpses of hope. We make money and maybe we save some. Yet the more we make and the more we save, the more we feel a pressure to make more and save more. Then, we spend money to replace time lost with what we truly cherish. We fail and fall short of these expectations; we lose a part of ourselves—hope crushed before our very eyes. Thus begins the endless spiral. In time, we become the hamster, running around the wheel, going nowhere.

You've heard it said: "He's living the good life." What is the good life, really? Is it fancy yachts? Big houses? Fast cars? Fine wines? If so, think again. There will always be fancier yachts, larger homes, faster cars, and finer wines.

Is it comfort? What is comfort? Living indoors? Running water? Air conditioning? Don't most of us have those things?

Yet, we're still searching.

What if the good life is a poor substitute for the life we were created to live?

As I continued to look, I saw that some people lived differently; their light seemed to come from somewhere else. It both puzzled and amazed me at the same time. They experienced pain but reacted differently. They didn't jump point to point searching for joy; they owned it. Contrary to popular belief, it didn't appear to have much to do with money. In fact, that was the beauty of it. It was something deeper—a richness from within.

As I began to seek insight and wisdom, the clouded glass started to become clear. There were people in my life who held no fear of death, as if their richness radiated from inside, giving them strength and purpose.

However, I also saw others who seemed hopeless. Fighting this battle with richness was leaving them battered and broken. Through the facade of the everyday, they were dying, and it terrified them. Their pursuit of richness was rooted in the world's definition. They would work, work, work in efforts to buy their life, their happiness. Spending money to live was their only way to avoid the inevitable. In a country founded on life, liberty, and the pursuit of happiness, they'd been told that happiness is a by-product of wealth, that joy is found in the abundance of possessions.

I know this because I was one of them. No matter the scale, this appeal is crippling for all of us. When we give in to this temptation, we become shackled.

Now, I must say that this book does not look upon money or financial well-being as unimportant. More so, the belief that money is, in any way, evil or bad. In fact, quite the opposite. It is the power that money can have over our lives that turns trivial pursuits into all-consuming purposes. If we begin to love money, it has the quick potential to unravel the very fabric of our lives—the power to consume our thoughts and wreck our emotions. It can destroy relationships, unhinge families, and corrupt even the strongest morals. Once this happens, we are but pawns, controlled by outside forces because we have given away our affections.

In regard to finances, the key word becomes *stewardship*—how well we care for, maintain, and grow that with which we have been entrusted. Money is a blessing to those who steward it well and view it with proper perspective; it is a curse to those who do not. Therefore, we must place it within that proper perspective. When viewed improperly, money calls to us on the basis of pride—the type of pride rooted in oneself and comparison. The dangerous type of pride is not that we covet someone else for having a certain thing; we covet the idea that they have more than us. Such is the same with money. However, when placed in its proper context, money becomes an incredible resource that can and will accomplish a great amount of good. A gift, not only for yourself, but for others as well.

This book isn't about finances. This book isn't about death. There are many quality books on both subjects. This book is about our choice. A choice to live richly.

Can we live in a way that transcends death?

Can we live a life far greater than we can conceive?

Do we all have hope for richness?

These are questions I've asked myself. I have felt my flame glow in the heat of hope, and I have seen it drenched in the sea of defeat. As I began to understand these truths in my life, I started reaching out to see if they existed in the lives of others. What I found simply confirmed the feelings I had been wresting inside.

I began asking people, "Tell me what richness means to you. Tell me your story."

What I've been met with has far exceeded anything I ever expected when I began writing. Stories of richness pouring over, blessing me in specific and measurable ways. Stories empowering me to live in pursuit of this new understanding of a word I had long misunderstood.

In this book, I will share those stories with you.

As I began writing, an experience from my past returned to mind, as if I were reliving it all over again. It had happened some six years earlier in a time of great sadness. I had recognized it at the time, but not in its full power. I heard the words, but it took me six years to see their truth. I now know this is where my journey began.

Death is inevitable. Life, well, that is up you. In the midst of telling this story, I discovered how to really live. I found a new perspective and roadway of the true life we all desire.

A life of richness.

CHAPTER 2

Finding Life in the Middle of Death

T ricia was a dreamer. She chose to look at all that life could be and, at every turn, celebrated the special moments. I guess you could say she was a romantic at heart, never letting the cloak of realism hinder her outlook. Every story had a happy ending, and every day brought new opportunity. She was a breath of fresh air, a welcomed break from the norm. People and ideas were met with her energy and excitement; even when she was diagnosed with cancer at forty-eight years of age, she dreamed big. Cancer wasn't going to stop her, and it certainly wasn't going to be an imposition on anyone else.

In fact, the year she was diagnosed, she took her thirty-eighth trip to Walt Disney World and relished it as if it were her first. To her, Disney embodied the way she lived, especially this part of her journey. In spite of her diagnosis, a hope grew within her, facing her condition as an opportunity rather than a burden.

Isn't this how every Disney movie seems? A story filled with tragedy: Mufasa dies attempting to save Simba, forcing the young cub to run away from his rightful throne; it appears as if Beauty can't quite save the Beast; Nemo finds himself torn from his father; and Andy's toys are seemingly separated once and for all.

We all know tragedy and struggle in one way or another, and it's discouraging when those characteristics weave a thread throughout our lives. However, according to every Disney story, resolution waits on the other side. Just when the situation seems utterly hopeless, tragedy is replaced by joy; defeat triumphed by victory.

Simba returns to Pride Rock to defeat his Uncle Scar and reclaim his position as king; Beauty falls in love with the Beast just as the last rose petal falls to the floor; Nemo and Marlin are happily reunited; and Andy's toys are rescued and find purpose in new friendships.[1]

In Tricia's mind, she knew her story would end happily ever after, just like every Disney movie she loved.

Aunt Trish had been that way as long as I could remember.

Shortly after I married my wife, Liz, we moved to Florida and established our life and our marriage on our own terms. Not in a defiant way, but we'd made the decision together to pursue a career opportunity that called us away from the comfort of home. Although we enjoyed being on our own, it was always a welcome treat to see family and friends.

So when Uncle Larry called to let me know that he and Aunt Trish were coming to Orlando, Liz and I excitedly made plans to meet them. After a short, two-hour drive, we arrived with great anticipation, ready for some quality family time.

Non-Hodgkin lymphoma is a form of cancer that attacks the lymph nodes and immune system. Although the sound of it seems ominous, it is actually one of the more curable forms of cancer, if there is such a thing. Just a couple of weeks before our visit, Uncle Larry and Aunt Trish almost canceled the trip. At the time, I wondered if something was going on. Quite honestly, marital problems were the first thing that came to mind. Not that Larry and Trish had a troubled marriage, but I knew how common marital strain was in the world around me, so my assumptions led me there.

Cancer was the last thing on my mind.

When we arrived, I immediately noticed that she and Larry interacted differently from what I was used to. Their energy, excitement, and laughter were abounding. Their lives seemed renewed, and there was a refreshing exchange between the two of them. Their glances and laughter carried a new spark. During our time together at Disney World that year, I saw their eyes fill with life as they embraced familiar joys. There was meaning, even in the mundane.

I'll never forget the night we made a grocery store run to stock our condo. The small, black BMW could hardly contain the four of us and our groceries. Surrounded by a mountain of the week's provisions, Trish poked her head through a hole among the bags, smiling the most cheerful of smiles, laughing out loud. I can still see her face surrounded by groceries with the biggest smile imaginable.

Neither Larry nor Trish ever spoke of her cancer during our time together. It wasn't until a few months later that they shared the news with the family. However, living more than six hundred miles away created a separation from the entire struggle that I wouldn't fully realize until later. Besides, Trish's story always ended happily in my mind, so I never considered that would be some of the last quality time I spent with her. A few visits home and scattered phone calls let me know that she was fighting her cancer battle as I expected, with courage, integrity, and inner strength. The prognosis was always great, so we had no reason to suspect otherwise. That was just Aunt Trish. She never wanted to be a burden. Actually, she wanted the opposite: she wanted to be a blessing.

It wasn't until the Christmas season in 2006 when we visited my hometown of Wilmington, North Carolina, to be with my family, that I even realized she was so sick. She was adamant on hosting a Christmas party. It was her chance to plan, produce, and serve the ones she loved the most. However, the pressure to cancel was real. At her request, no one was to know she had been given a terminal diagnosis earlier that month. The treatments were not working, and her cancer was spreading. Trish was dying. Yet, in the midst of this devastating news, she wanted to host a party—her party.

I vividly remember her moving around the house with her wig and Christmas sweater in full flair. The spread was second to none, and the homemade eggnog was at its best. Everything seemed as it always was. Except for Trish. I saw the weakness in her face and noticed that her efforts were taking their toll on her body, particularly her breathing. Even in dying, she never let it stop her from living. In fact, it was likely that party that caused her to spend Christmas Eve in the hospital. Much to her chagrin, the doctors insisted she rest. It drove her crazy, and she begged to get out Christmas morning, refusing to miss our family tradition at my grandmother's home. Her breathing was better, so the doctors obliged. However, the following week, she was forced to return.

Liz and I had since moved to Columbia, South Carolina, and had just left Wilmington after the holidays when I received a call from my Uncle Larry. "If you want to see your aunt, now's the time."

The weight of those words rested like a boulder upon my chest. However, there was still hope within me. *This is just the bad part of the movie*, I would tell myself as I refused to come to grips with the reality that was unfolding. *This is the part right before the miracle occurs.* My drive back home was heavy with questions.

Why Aunt Trish? Disney stories aren't supposed to end this way.

Why so young? She had a daughter to raise and a life to live. It all seemed so unfair.

When I arrived at the hospital, I immediately met the truth head-on. I knew now why my uncle had called me. Until this point, I had held on to every last ounce of hope to the promise of life and healing for my aunt. The promise that all stories end happily. It was then that I finally realized Aunt Trish was dying, and I felt like someone had taken a sledgehammer to my heart. I was Trish's first nephew and, while I'm not implying I was her favorite by any stretch, we did have a unique bond.

The lobby waiting room was filled with familiar faces, none wanting to meet under these circumstances. We avoided eye contact with each other as a way to delay the inevitable. Anxious to visit with Aunt Trish, I made my way into her room.

Hospital lighting carries a unique glow. That night, it conveyed a mood of its own. It wasn't bright, but at the same time, it wasn't dark. It was an inviting glow that seemed to encircle Trish as she lie in her bed. The rest of the room held darkness that I would associate with death, but not with Trish. The light fell upon her. Across the room, I could see her slouched over a pillow, wheezing for air. Her cancer had spread throughout her chest cavity, and now she was retaining fluid. Her cancer was suffocating her.

When I caught her eye, she lit up as usual and in a weak but joyful voice said, "Hey, Matt Matt!" Her eyes, peering through her glasses, still carried a spark. I was used to seeing her in contacts. The glasses, along with the effects of her illness, made her look older, but her eyes were no different. Always vibrant and full of life. Her face was swollen due to her fluid retention, but nothing could hide her smile.

She didn't speak much, as it required energy she no longer had. I did most of the talking. You never know what to say to someone faced with the nearness of death; at least, I do not. I'm certain there are words that are better than others, but I talked mostly of our collective faith in God and my love for her; expressing gratitude for her presence in my life for the previous twenty-five years. We reminisced about the time we danced in my family's kitchen at Thanksgiving. As the turkey roasted in the oven, we played beach music and used the time to dance. Honestly, it was the time together that we remembered. The time together that mattered. I was content to just sit by her bedside.

As we sat there, a nurse stepped in to help Trish get comfortable. I realized it was just the three of us in the room, and I thought this odd, considering how many others were in the waiting room, and I expected someone else to step in at any moment. However, no one did, which now adds even more significance to the moment.

What happened next is cemented in my mind as one of those life-altering experiences—an undeniable moment, despite all efforts to make it seem "normal."

Aunt Trish was visibly weak. Her wheezing was causing her to tire, and the nurse gently propped her up between breaths. I watched these events unfold like I wasn't even in the room. I was simply witnessing something profound, without any participation of my own. As the nurse leaned in to straighten her pillow, Trish grabbed a deep breath. As her chest lifted, her body followed. She used that breath to muster enough energy, look at her nurse, and say, "You make my life easy." Without hesitation, the nurse smiled and graciously, yet confidently, responded.

"You make my life rich."

I repeated those words in my mind, not fully understanding what they meant.

You make my life rich.

I felt like God placed an angel from heaven in that moment to deliver those words. I have no idea who that nurse was, but what she said sent shockwaves through my soul. Even as I write about it now, I'm taken back to that hospital room, my perspective that of an onlooker, observing the moment from the sidelines, like watching a movie of my own life. The most incredible part to me is that no one else was there to hear those words. Despite the gallery of loved ones just outside the door, no one else entered. It was just Aunt Trish, the nurse, and me.

Other than my own good-bye as I left the room, those were the last words I heard spoken to Trish. She died the next morning.

Over the next few days, the mourning set in for our family. Our beloved Trish was gone. As a means of comfort, I shared the story of our exchange with the family. At the time, those words provided consolation, but in the middle of our loss, we never saw their truth. They simply gave us peace in the midst of a very difficult time. In fact, Uncle Larry asked me if I would say a few words at the funeral some days later. During her eulogy, I alluded to the nurse's words. I was mourning the loss of my aunt and trying to understand why the story didn't end the way I thought it would; I never knew how that story began to come to life. After the service, countless friends and family members approached me with encouragement, saying, "Matt, you have to share that story."

I graciously thanked them and never gave it any further thought. Quite honestly, I was twenty-five at the time, and my definition of what it meant to be rich was my own. I was trying to build richness according to the world's standards and, also, I missed my aunt. Those struggles held the truth captive. Only now have I come to realize the power they hold. It took six years for them to rest upon my heart and many life experiences before they would be brought to life again. Now, with the clarity that hindsight offers, I understand Trish needed those words. Those words gave her strength in her most vulnerable moment. More importantly, those words gave her peace. That exchange with the nurse was in no way trite or patronizing —those were words of dignity, grace, and depth.

You make my life rich.

I now know my presence in the hospital room that day was not coincidental, and those words weren't just for Trish, but for me as well.

And, maybe, those words were for you too.

CHAPTER 3

Death and Life

It has been said that death is the great equalizer, something we all face, regardless of our willingness. We hear it all the time: *you're not guaranteed tomorrow.* Yet, we brush it off, not wanting to face that possibility. As I look around, I see that people have a real fear of death. People don't want to plan for it and instead refuse to wrestle with their own mortality. For something so certain, it always comes as a surprise. Many people will not even discuss it.

My career as an insurance agent has taught me this lesson well. Most clients are eager and willing to talk about their insurance needs in regard to their home and auto protection. However, when I bring up life insurance, the mood usually changes completely. Avoidance sets in, and excuses become commonplace. People don't want to discuss it because they don't want to consider the possibility in their own lives. Even as you read this, you may become uncomfortable and fidgety.

Death is something beyond our comprehension and is shrouded in uncertainty. I don't think death is something to dwell on, but I don't think it is something to fear either. As Mufasa shared with young Simba in Disney's *The Lion King*, it is part of the circle of life.

As I started unpacking this, I felt overwhelmed with our culture's fear of death. Tim McGraw's "Live Like You Were Dying" paints a picture of people waiting until they get a diagnosis to start living. He sings of a man "looking at the X-rays and talking about sweet time." The chorus closes with the line, "Some day I hope you get the chance to live like you were dying."[1] That is a tragic thought to me: waiting until the end to live the life we desire. Why should it take a terminal diagnosis for people to understand that they can live this way? I think Tim McGraw's encouragement is mine as well; certainly, there has to be a different way.

I recalled that hospital room, and I found the answer.

So many people are afraid of dying because they haven't really lived. When Trish was told, "You make my life rich," she received affirmation. As I said, those words provided her comfort and peace. Now I see they also afforded her the perspective that her death, although tragic, was not without purpose. Her death was not in vain. I think those words showed her that, even at forty-nine, she had lived a great life. She had lived richly and shared her riches with others. The nurse knew that. She absorbed Trish's radiant grace and dignity, and the result was richness. She didn't say, "Thank you" or "You make my life easy too." That nurse said, "You make my life rich." It was the perfect exchange in the perfect moment that gave me a context to understand one of the deep mysteries of life. In my mind, those words allowed Trish to rest eternally.

It wasn't until I started writing this book and shared this idea with my uncle that I knew this was true. When I told him about the story and what I had begun to write, he shared with me that just before she died, Trish said, "We had a good run, didn't we." This wasn't a question; it was a statement. Trish knew she had lived richly and somewhere within, she knew her journey was just beginning.

It's a Wonderful Life

We all know Frank Capra's 1946 classic movie *It's a Wonderful Life*. Most of us catch the film around the holidays, as its final scenes are set during Christmastime. The film takes place in the town of Bedford Falls, a small, simple community that gives the impression the story could take place anywhere. The great James Stewart plays the lead character, George Bailey.

Bailey has aspirations for a great life. To him, this life consists of traveling the world, seeing marvelous sights, and experiencing grandeur that Bedford Falls cannot offer. However, after the financial crisis of the Great Depression and the death of his father, George finds himself putting his life on hold to run the family Savings and Loan. In his own mind, he never gets to live his dream—his dream of richness.

As the story unfolds, he runs into a financial crisis of his own after his uncle misplaces a bank deposit. Convinced he is better off dead, George yells at his family and storms out of his house, distraught and hopeless. He heads for a bridge on that icy night. Cursing God for the life he's lived and the situation he's facing, he's reached his final straw. As he contemplates his own life, hope appears in the form of a guardian angel, Clarence. Clarence arrives from above to give George a glimpse of his importance: the opportunity to experience the way the world might have been if he had never existed. As George travels to this alternate world, much to his dismay, the town of Bedford Falls has been run under by an old miser. Mr. Potter's Pottersville is nothing like the town he knew and loved. His mother is an old widow, and his wife is a lonely, unmarried librarian. His children do not exist.

This vision terrifies him, and he looks up to God, pleading, "Take me back! I want to live again!" As he comes out of his revelation, George is a new man as he has seen, in great detail, the wonderful life he lives and the difference he has made in the lives of his family and his community. He runs through town shouting with joy, then rushing home to embrace his family. As he realizes that he is still in his financial predicament, he is surrounded by friends and family who have come to his aid. His perspective has changed, his life renewed. His friends begin to pour into his living room and dump loads of money into a basket. Everyone has come together to help George in his time of need. Then, his little brother, Harry, bursts through the door declaring the line that resonates so deeply.

"Cheers to my big brother George, the richest man in town!"[2]

I believe the success of *It's a Wonderful Life* is due to the fact that it reminds us of our own conditions. We question whether we've lived a wonderful life. It confirms what we know, yet refuse to believe. A great, wonderful life has everything to do with being rich, and being rich has very little to do with money.

Material possessions and financial well-being are simply a matter of perspective when someone embraces true riches. However, our world is consumed with this pursuit of material wealth. We are a society and a culture searching for life, longing for meaning and purpose. On every television station, reality shows portray the masses chasing their own version of richness. Most are riddled with disaster and failure, regardless of whether they get their riches or not.

I've found that people who desire richness take one of two paths.

There is the path of material abundance and luxury, the one reality television offers us. People running themselves ragged chasing a dream of riches. These people place their desire for wealth in the forefront of their minds, but it leads them into a comparison trap. When it comes to quantifying riches, someone always has more. Richer. Stronger. Smarter. Prettier. These comparisons leave people striving, longing to reach an unreachable goal.

The other path is that of those who have a desire for riches but are paralyzed by fear; they're scared to pursue it themselves. They would rather sit back and watch someone else hurt than actually run the risk of hurting. I think this explains the success of reality television. It's not only watching someone else hurt, but their pain subconsciously reminds us of our own, and then consciously masks it from us. Additionally, the folks in this category may run from riches altogether, declaring it the great evil in the world. It's not a fear of it, but rather a distaste.

Ultimately, both roads lead to a dead end. We are all searching for life abundant, but our metric has become skewed.

Is there another way?

I'm learning that the good life we've come to know has been tarnished over the years with a facade of fallacy. The good life we talk about isn't the good life after all.

The more I talk with people, the more I believe this to be true. I've heard too many retirees lament, "I did all of that for this?" I've seen too many wealthy people lose everything looking for something more.

Is there another path to richness that we can experience?

Maybe we have the right word, but the wrong definition. Maybe we should pursue richness with an understanding of its deeper meaning. Maybe we should redefine rich.

Abounding in Desirable Qualities

As I sat down to write, those words shared some six years earlier by the nurse with no name were painted neon on my heart, "You make my life rich."

What do those words mean?

I grabbed a dictionary and stared at numerous definitions of the word rich, most notably the common understanding.

Rich: financial well-being.

However, I continued reading and saw this definition:

Rich: abounding in desirable qualities.

> **Rich:** adj., richer, richest. [3]
>
> 1. of great value or worth;
> 2. abounding in desirable qualities;
> 3. abundant, plentiful, or ample.

It nearly jumped off the page at me. What a great aspiration, to abound in desirable qualities. As I reread it, I knew there was something there. When we look at history, great men and women didn't risk their lives to fight for material abundance; they declared freedom and fought for life abundant. That's where my journey was to begin. Somewhere within that explanation was the definition Trish had come to understand the night before she died. That is the definition George Bailey experienced. That is the definition I want so deeply to understand. As I seek to explain what I've come to know, I'll start with a few questions.

Can we all live a life abounding in desirable qualities?

Can we all live richly?

If so, what would that look like?

Quite frankly, I believe it has almost nothing to do with finances, but at the same time, I believe it can have everything to do with them when we begin to understand a deeper point of view. Again, the acquiring and possession of wealth are not bad things in and of themselves. Hard work and responsible wealth management are respectable and necessary traits. It's these desirable qualities and the leveraging of them that give us the choice to respond in any situation. The ability to live our life instead of it living us.

In the end, if we all had the option to choose words that would be said to us on our death bed, doesn't "You make my life rich" sound like words we would choose? Wouldn't they be the mark of a wonderful life?

The truth, I believe, is that we are all in a process of growing and becoming. We are all moving in one direction or another: toward richness or away from it. Therefore, richness isn't a destination we arrive at—it's a process of living that we must come to understand.

CHAPTER 4

The Ground Rules

Growing up as a baseball player, I learned the importance of what are called the *ground rules.* These ground rules exist as a way to explain certain nuances of the game as they apply to each individual ballpark. Some fields have dugouts that are below the surface of the field while others are contained within a fence. Thus, each field has its own set of rules as they apply to its individual circumstances. I find the same to be true as we tackle this concept of richness. The ground rules will help us understand a few things that are important before we begin to play the game.

First of all, it is important to understand that this book isn't for everyone.

If you say, *I've got it all together; I'm exactly where I want to be,* you won't find much help here. However, if there is a spark inside of you that wonders what it would be like to live differently, to live *richly*, I look forward to walking with you.

Before we launch into the principles that help us redefine rich, there are two key components to understand and grasp. I call these the ground rules and I want to help frame them for you.

1. You can live a rich life.

2. It will not happen by accident.

The Culture of Can't

It's easy, dare I say comfortable, to believe, *I can't live a rich life. You don't understand my story; you don't know the situation I'm in.* Circumstances are often overwhelming, paralyzing us from making necessary changes. We are held captive by our present situations, stuck in the cycle of habit.

The word *can't* is a very dangerous one. If we fail to acknowledge this danger, we slip into a belief system where it is widely used and accepted. *Can't* squashes hope, and hope is the very thing opportunity is made of. *Can't* limits possibility and draws us into thinking from a negative perspective, rather than a positive one. I've found that most successful people hate the word *can't*, as they refuse to limit themselves. Instead, they consider what is possible and approach life from a more positive angle, a fresh perspective.

Michael Jordan and I have similar stories. Well, at least our beginnings do. As you may know, Michael Jordan, arguably the greatest basketball player of all time, was cut from his high school basketball team. Jordan attended Laney High School in our shared hometown of Wilmington, North Carolina, and as a sophomore, he was cut from the squad.

He was told he simply couldn't play. Can you image the hope-crushing blow those words delivered him? Fourteen-year-olds are vulnerable enough already, but how much more so upon receiving an emphatic *can't* in regard to chasing a dream?

As Jordan has shared so many times, it was that comment that catapulted his motivation for greatness. It was hearing *can't* that caused him to work even harder to achieve his potential. He used the time to practice and strengthen his game, working on every facet that would cause him to become a champion. The rest is history. In his 1994 book, *I Can't Accept Not Trying*, Jordan says, "I can accept failure; everyone fails at something. But I can't accept not trying."[1] The power of positive affirmation reminds me that *can't* doesn't belong in the vocabulary of someone longing for true richness.

Like Jordan, I played in my driveway growing up in Wilmington. It was hard to be from the same hometown and not love Jordan's story. His pictures were plastered all across town, and occasionally he would come back to visit. The streets would buzz, announcing, "Mike's in town!"

I never really played competitive basketball, as baseball was my sport, but by middle school, I found myself playing pick-up during gym class. As I began competing on more than a recreational level, I began thinking, *Maybe I'll play basketball.* I went to our coach and told him my thoughts.

I received a devastating response, very similar to Jordan's: *You can't play basketball. You're too slow. You'll never play in high school. Stick to baseball.*

I didn't know what to say or what to think. I was crushed. Now, I knew I wasn't God's gift to basketball, and yes, I was slow, but *can't* and *never*? I was defeated. I met this defeat with a normal but useless response: non-action. I feared the rejection my coach already suspected, so I didn't even try out. I was paralyzed by my fear. That is what *can't* does; it lets fear creep in to do its work.

Fast-forward a couple of years. I continued to play recreationally and by the tenth grade, a couple of guys on the high school junior varsity team told me that I should try out. Instinctively, I echoed the coach's words to me.

"I'm too slow to play, guys; I'm a baseball player." My fear trapped me in its deceptive web.

However, I started battling with my *can't*. Somewhere inside me there was still a flicker of hope. I recalled Jordan's story and similar encouragement, causing me to change my approach. I listened to Jordan; I had to try. I let my *can't* become *Can I?*

Can: auxiliary verb [2]

1. to be able to;

2. have the ability, power, or skill to.

Here is how I would encourage you to fight *can't* in your life. Instead of believing you *can't*, do something new. It is a simple pivot in your approach to any challenge. Turn it into a question.

Ask yourself *if* you can: *Can I?* Because even though you may be uncertain, a positive question will empower you, at least a seed of belief. Don't squash belief with *can't*.

My *Can I?* motivated me to act. I tried out and made the junior varsity team. Not only did I make the team, I started. Not only did I start, I was moved up to varsity after just a few games.

Here's the interesting part. The first game I played in was

against our cross-town rival, Laney High School—the same school Jordan attended years before. In their gym, a giant mural of Michael Jordan graces the wall behind the basket. When Coach called my name to enter the game, I sat by the scorer's table, waiting for a stoppage in play. As I sat there, I looked at the mural and thought, *Thanks, Mike.*

The same slow kid who would never play in high school was playing varsity basketball two years later as a sophomore. I hadn't grown six inches and I hadn't gotten any faster; it was my belief in myself and then learning to harness my strengths. I was a big guy who played the post; good for rebounds, put-backs, and fouls. Much to the dismay of my opponents, I learned how to foul effectively. As they say, "You've got five to give." I leveraged those strengths and ended up a co-captain my senior year, starting every game.

Here's the funny thing about hope: when you learn to live with it, it has a way of reminding you it's there. Remember the coach who told me, "You'll never play in high school"? He took a coaching job at my high school my senior year. On senior night, four years after he said those infamous words, he lined the tunnel with the other coaches as we ran out on the floor. I went up to him before the game and reminded him of our exchange. I didn't do this to rub it in his face; I actually said it as a *thank you* for the motivation he gave me. And thanks to Michael Jordan, I replaced my *can't* with *Can I?*

I challenge you to do the same.

Somewhere along the road to your rich life, you might stop seeking possibility and settle for *can't.* I know I have. Maybe you already have too. Do you let this contraction rule your life? How many times have you said, *"I can't do that"*? Better yet, has someone ever told you, *"You can't do that"*? How have you responded?

Now I understand that there are some physical limitations, but push through them. Physically impossible feats like flying or breathing under water have been accomplished by people pushing those boundaries. Air travel and SCUBA diving both came into being because someone pushed the boundary of possibility by asking *Can I?* Extraordinary things begin by asking simple questions. The best example of this in my own life comes from my young sons.

Having three boys at and under the age of four has the power to limit your vocabulary to three words: *No, Don't,* and *Stop!* Every moment my boys are exploring, even though it seems like impending doom hovers, waiting to strike. What I have come to realize is that their lives are powered by the words *Can* and *Can I?* This of course isn't just my children, but *all* children. They find possibilities in everything as they explore their world. There are childish ways that we need to grow out of, but this isn't one of them. The beauty is found in that moment when *Can I?* becomes *I Can!* Children thrive in their accomplishment as possibilities increase. I can hear their precious screams now, *"Look at me, Daddy!"* This is the process of learning and growing. This is what we seek.

Ask yourself this question:

Can I live a rich life?

If you start pushing the boundaries of possibility in your life, you will be amazed at what you can do.

Understanding Intentionality:
It Will Not Happen on Accident

Before we get started on the principles that will help us redefine rich, we must understand ground rule number two:

a rich life does not happen on accident. The good news is that if you're reading this book, you're already on your way. You've taken action based on a suggestion, and that is where it starts. The suggestion may have come from a friend or it may have come from something inside of you. That is the voice of intentionality. Carrying through on those suggestions will help you discover the path you are to follow.

The point is, a rich life is created by living intentionally, living on purpose.

You may have noticed that I ask a lot of questions. Questions are imperative. I've heard it said and believe it fully, "The quality of your life is determined by the quality of questions in it." If you're questioning and you're searching, you're moving in an intentional direction. To accept the status quo tethers you to average. Richness is far beyond average. It's purposeful.

It doesn't matter if you are a stay-at-home mom or the family breadwinner, married or not married, employee or employer; everyone has a purpose and everyone can be great. The Bible tells us in Genesis that we were created in the image of God, in the image of the Creator himself. Regardless of your view of faith, we can agree that no one was created for mediocrity or put here on earth to fail. No one sets out to dream small. But if you fail to live intentionally, you may become the person you never meant to be.

> **Intentional**: adj. [3]
> 1.   done with intention or on purpose.

You see, intentions are dangerous because they lull us into a belief system in which we value our hearts instead of our actions. People often say, "I'm a good person," but this is a belief about themselves based on their intentions. All too often, this declaration is strikingly different from reality, isn't it? Intentions are necessary because they are the objects of our purpose and vision; but alone, they are useless.

I once made the mistake of telling my wife on her birthday, "I meant to send you flowers." I really did; I thought about it, planned it out, and even wrote down the florist's phone number. Then I totally forgot to make the call. My intentions were there; shouldn't that be enough? I loved and appreciated my wife and I wanted to do something to show her. I thought mentioning it in conversation would just show that I cared. Care to guess how that one went over?

I cared enough to think about you.

That sounds incredibly silly, but it's the way we think sometimes. How rude of us to expect everyone else to understand and supremely value our intentions. We must understand that it is our action—based on our intention—that gets things going. The problem is that most of us have great intentions; we simply don't act in agreement with them. At the end of the day, it really doesn't matter what your intentions alone are because no one can see them; they lay powerless without action. However, when combined with action, intentions create influence. It takes action to set the wheels of intention rolling, and the results are powerful. By living intentionally, we start thinking and acting on purpose, which moves us in a certain direction. In short, it helps our *Can I?* become *I Can.*

As we take our first steps, remember the ground rules. Simply put:

You can, and it's up to you.

CHAPTER 5

A Visual Aid—The RICH Acrostic

Now that we've covered the ground rules, it's time to uncover the characteristics of a rich life. When I first sat down with this idea, I was consumed with all of the potential traits. However, four significant trends really came into focus as I started pouring over the stories I encountered, all fitting neatly into one context. A good frame of reference not only sets expectations, but it gives us a roadmap to follow. Additionally, it helps us work on the process one step at a time. We all know the old adage, "How do you eat an elephant?" That's right: "One bite at a time."

As a visual person, I love acronyms and acrostics. I remember them vividly from my school days as tools to help me learn certain concepts. For example, to remember the main notes of a musical scale, we use the acronym:

Every
Good
Boy
Does
Fine

Do you remember these? Since ancient times, this method has been used to help with reference and memorization. I think it will be a great tool for us as well.

As I placed the four principles I found into this context, I saw them tuck perfectly into the word itself. I have come up with an acrostic for the word *rich* that will help us walk through the process of defining a rich life. Additionally, it will give you this frame of reference as you remember and implement the principles we will discuss.

Here they are:

Recognize you're broke[n]
Invest in others
Choose gratitude
Humble yourself with confidence

These four principles will guide us on our path of living richly. I believe my Aunt Trish lived in a way that allowed her nurse to see the richness inside her. More importantly, I believe the nurse embodied certain principles as well, allowing her to see richness as it radiated before her. By sharing those words with my aunt, the nurse allowed Trish to see them in herself as well. The essence of the principles was framed within the context of that word: *rich*. This mutual understanding between my aunt and her nurse provided clarity, peace, and hope, in spite of the circumstances.

Let's begin implementing these four steps into our journey.

Part Two
The Four Principles of Richness

CHAPTER 6

Principle 1–Recognize You're Broke[n]

Completely Broken:
The Redeeming Story of Gary Weller

Gary Weller has every reason to pin blame. He was an active, athletic man, full of life and energy. The majority of his adult life was spent engaging his passions, football and people, earning him the affectionate title of Coach. Coach was well known and well respected in his community, as he spent fourteen years running the sideline, coaching his players as the head football coach of Pine Forest High School in Fayetteville, North Carolina.

On April 14, 2004, a beautiful spring day, Coach dropped his car off at the mechanic and decided to jog home. This was a common practice, something he'd done numerous times before. Even at fifty-five, he remained in great physical shape; a quality that would likely save his life.

Donning a blue windbreaker, he set off on the four-mile trek that would lead him home. Despite the opposition from his wife and his mechanic, who both offered to give him a ride, he carried out his plan.

Coach was a very alert runner, always assessing his terrain. As he ran that day, he noticed a utility van making a U-turn in the parking lot to his right. As he passed by, he was unaware that this particular city utility van was stolen and driven by a deranged man intent on running down men, using the van as his weapon. Coach was his next victim.

Moments later, Weller was hit from behind as the driver veered some thirty feet, intentionally striking his victim and dragging him over a hundred feet underneath the van. As the tire marks across his blue windbreaker would later testify, the driver backed over his motionless victim before speeding away. Slipping in and out of consciousness, Coach knew death was certain.

The attack left Weller with fractures too numerous to count. First responders would later comment that the physical condition of his body was unlike anything they had ever seen; he was almost unrecognizable. Weller would be resuscitated four times before being airlifted to UNC-Chapel Hill Hospital, where he would lie hopelessly unconscious, comatose for thirty-five days. His wife, Cathy, would later say that those thirty-five days were the most difficult of her life.

Miraculously, and despite tire marks across his chest, Coach suffered no spinal cord injuries and no permanent brain damage. Yet, in his own words, he was completely broken. Physically, emotionally, and spiritually broken. As he awoke from his coma, he became aware of his grave condition.

Coach admits, "I was mad; this wasn't my vision for my life."

Determined to talk to everyone on the scene, Coach began asking questions to better grasp the situation and discover some measure of understanding. In those conversations, he realized the only understanding was that he should be dead. In fact, the next victim of the deranged driver tragically bled to death on the scene. Gary Weller shouldn't be alive.

Coach Weller spent over two years on his back recovering from his wounds, which left him but a shadow of his former, physically fit self. Actually, the physical condition his body was in at the time led to his ability to battle back from his brokenness. Two years spent lying on your back gives you plenty of time to think, plenty of time to become bitter. However, Coach chose a different path. He understood he was broken for a reason.

Weller's physical brokenness was unmistakable. Through remarkable surgeries, his body was able to heal, and although he was limited physically, his body was not crushed. Neither was his spirit. His spiritual and emotional brokenness could have yielded a bitter, broken man. However, he made a choice—a choice to respond. During the capital murder trial, Coach verbally forgave his attacker.

How is that possible? How could he forgive?

In his own words, Coach said, "I refused to be bent up with bitterness."

He understood that forgiveness was a necessary tool in repairing brokenness.

Without forgiveness, wounds cannot fully heal, as forgiveness is the catalyst for the healing of the spirit. Without forgiveness, anger secures a foothold. If you're not careful, it will make a home in your soul, crippling it for eternity.

Weller, now sixty-five, is ten years removed from the tragic events that forever shaped his life. He is bound to a wheelchair, only able to stand with the support of a walker, but he doesn't let his physical ability limit him. He travels locally in eastern North Carolina, speaking to groups with empowering words, a story that shapes lives, and mottos like, "A bad attitude is like a flat tire; you've gotta change it if you want to get where you're going."

In short, he coaches them. He uses his brokenness and healing to heal the hearts of others.

I recently had the privilege of hearing Coach speak, and then the opportunity to interview him as part of my journey to understanding true richness. In our time together, he shared these words from Garth Brooks' beautiful song "The River." It was these words that encouraged him as he recovered:

There's bound to be rough waters and I know I'll take some falls But with the good Lord as my Captain I can make it through them all[1]

As you walk your path to healing, and as you wrestle with forgiveness, amazing things will happen. You will be given opportunities to heal those wounds in ways you would never imagine.

A few years after his recovery, Coach was attending a class reunion for his son. His story preceded him, and one of his son's classmates was actually the wife of Weller's attending surgeon in the ER the night of his accident. The surgeon had not planned on going, but he heard Coach would be there and wanted to meet him himself. As the ER surgeon approached Weller and told him who he was, both were overcome with emotion. As they hugged and wept, Coach simply said *thank you* through his tears.

The ER physician looked right into Weller's eyes and said, "Don't thank me; I just do God's work."

Rich words indeed.

Understanding Brokenness

Interestingly enough, the personal richness we seek carries so many similarities to financial richness that it's no wonder their pursuits are so often confused. For example, a desire to be wealthy only comes out of a place of financial trouble. For instance, if you're already wealthy, it wouldn't be something to aspire to, right? So, likewise, the desire to be truly rich must start with an acknowledgment that you're not. The first principle in living richly is:

R: *Recognize you're broke[n]*

Those words still sting me as I'm sure they do you. Who wants to admit that they're broken?

Broken: adj. [2]
1. reduced to fragments;
2. ruptured; torn; fractured.
3. not functioning properly; out of working order.

You see, we create a facade in our lives—a protective shield—where everything looks nice and neat from the outside. Everything has the appearance of richness, but below the surface, we wither away. There's poverty within, which we want to avoid at all cost. This is so true with financial wealth as well. We have *stuff*, but we leveraged ourselves to the hilt to get it. Car loans, school loans, and credit cards are all ways to cover up for a lack of financial prowess. In those instances, we're not wealthy; we are broke, and we just don't want to admit it. However, the truth of it in my own life has allowed me to see that the condition is universal. If we're not careful, we start to believe the facade rather than face our reality. This process of understanding brokenness is necessary to obtain the outcome of living richly. In fact, I think we need to work on being broken as a way to grow. Much like someone aspiring for wealth will work to earn money, we must work to learn brokenness. And trust me, it takes work.

Here's the tension. The world says, *You aren't broken; you're fine. It's just a phase.* If you're not broken or refuse to recognize your own brokenness, then we really can't get anywhere. However, if there's even a fraction of a percent of you that would indulge me, carry on.

Having three boys, I knew the day would come when I had to deal with broken bones; I was just hoping it would be delayed a bit. From an early age, my aspirations of becoming a doctor were quickly derailed when I realized how I responded to injuries. When it comes to bloody and broken, I'm not your guy. I know I'm destroying my manhood here, but I'm laying a foundation of honesty.

Just recently, my three-year-old, Matthew, whom we affectionately call MJ, fell from the couch and broke his left arm just above the elbow. Given my admitted weakness, I'm not sure who this experience was more traumatic for, him or me. It was the first time I had really seen him hurt. In fact, when he hit the ground, his cry was unique, one I had never heard before. We had dealt with bumps, bruises, viruses, and the occasional tantrum of an emotional overload, but never this. His response was full of fear as he tried to figure out as to why it hurt like it did. The pain wasn't stopping, and he was doubly upset because he couldn't go to a friend's birthday party later that day. Of course, he screamed through his tears as we loaded him up for the doctor. "Daddy, I want to go to the birthday party!" he sobbed.

Forgive me for using my three-year-old's pain as an example, but there is a great correlation here. Don't we all have a proverbial birthday party we long to go to, but there is something broken in our path? There is a dream that is covered in broken promises. A longing within, shattered by broken relationships. However, those realities create a condition. That condition is the only thing that allows for healing.

Going through this experience with MJ showed me that you can't fix something that isn't broken. The condition of brokenness is the only thing that allows the process of healing. Better yet, the recognition of something broken is the first step in moving toward a process of healing.

You see, ignoring our broken situations doesn't allow them to heal correctly. Adversely, understanding that you're broken has to be the first step in living richly because without it, there is no foundation. Healing correctly creates a foundation that we can build our richness upon.

I have a friend who broke his finger playing baseball thirty years ago. He never allowed his finger to fully heal, and now, it looks more like a talon. The bone grew back incorrectly, and his finger shows the history of the wound—a painful memory of his brokenness. In your own life, if you try to let a wound heal on its own, the scar will only remind you of the wound, instead of a place that has been healed.

In my experience, this has been the toughest principle to understand, but it is only through pain that we can heal. It is only through adversity that we can grow. As Gary Weller's life so beautifully illustrates, if we refuse to allow our wounds to heal, they will create hardened places in our hearts that won't allow proper growth. I picture talons on our hearts from the wounds that haven't healed properly. Doesn't it feel that way? But that's okay. Recognition is just the first step, and there's a natural process that our bodies go through when dealing with brokenness that brings us this truth.

Have you ever heard the phrase, "A broken bone heals stronger than it was before"? It's a common phrase, and the understanding of it is remarkable. As I looked into this real-life phenomenon during MJ's healing process, I found that this phrase is actually true; his bone was healing stronger than it was before. In a New York Times article from 2010, Dr. Terry D. Amaral, director of pediatric orthopedic surgery at Montefiore Medical Center in Bronx, New York, says, "The area that's healing is undergoing rapid mineralization, but because you can't use it, the rest of the bone is demineralized."[3] As a result, there is a period where the fracture is stronger.

Can you imagine?

In the process of healing, a bone is actually stronger than it was before it was broken. During the healing process, the calcium and minerals being deposited give the broken area an incredible amount of strength. And beautifully, after the break, the bone is the same as it was before. Therefore, our natural world proves that brokenness produces strength. It is not simply a cliché intended for a motivational poster on someone's wall; it is a fact of nature that we can rest in. Take heart knowing that your brokenness can make you stronger.

Broken Breakout

I love Dave Ramsey's story. As you may or may not know, Dave is the author of many books, most notably *Financial Peace* and *The Total Money Makeover*. Dave employees more than four hundred staff in his Nashville headquarters as they help millions of people take control of their finances. Dave hosts a self-titled radio talk show where listeners call in and walk through their situations of being broke as they seek financial peace. The best part of the show is when success stories are shared over the air as folks yell, "We're debt free!" Dave calls this the debt-free scream, and if you've never heard it, please take a listen to the show; it's incredibly powerful. However, Dave's story didn't start there. I recently attended one of Dave's live events and heard him give his testimony. As I listened, I saw that he had been broke; both personally and financially.[4]

By twenty-eight years of age, Dave had amassed a multi-million dollar business in real estate, yet he was very heavily leveraged with debt. During that time, some of the banks holding Dave's loans started calling them due. In his own words, "They saw a twenty-eight-year-old kid with over three million dollars in debt and said, 'We want our money now.'" Over a period of eighteen months, Dave and his wife Sharon lost everything they had, having to declare bankruptcy with young children at home. Most people would be devastated. Most people would have seen this as the end of the road. Sadly, many in this situation have made it the end of their road.

However, Dave used this experience as an incredible learning opportunity.

That's what rich people do. They use adversity and brokenness as an opportunity to learn. Their struggles don't define them; their response does. Dave decided on a few key steps that he had neglected and began again with the wisdom obtained through his brokenness. He began teaching his *baby steps* through financial classes and published his book, *Financial Peace,* which became a *New York Times* bestseller and has since sold millions of copies. More importantly, Dave uses his experience to inspire others.

When Dave speaks to his audience, he's speaking from experience. He was broken, and it was acknowledging his brokenness and his mistakes that allowed him to heal. I admire him immensely and admire what he does. As he says, "Live like no one else so later you can live like no one else."

Discovering Brokenness

So, where do you find your own brokenness?

That may be a question that requires some digging, but for most of us, we don't have to dig at all. We know our weaknesses and our wounds all too well. They are painful reminders throughout our past that bring back the brokenness we long to forget. Even when we feel like they're gone, they'll rear their heads in a painful reminder. We often don't need to look too far. We simply look to our scars.

We avoid their sting all too often. We try to let these broken places heal on their own, and we're left with scars that remind of us of our past, our wounds. We see this reiterated in pop culture. Adele's monumental hit "Rolling in the Deep" says it this way,

> *The scars of your love remind me of us. They keep me thinking that we almost had it all.* [5]

That's not just a great line from a beautiful singer; it's completely the point. Our scars remind us of our wounds when we don't let them heal correctly. For some of us, there are specific, single events that left us devastated. For others, it's many small events that culminate in a loss of hope. As the saying goes, "Death by a thousand cuts." In either case, one thing remains: a broken area. Now understand, these scars aren't always physical; oftentimes, they're emotional. Most of the time, the scars that can't be seen hide the deepest wounds.

I hear you saying, "Gee, Matt, thanks for reminding me." Please hang with me here. Remember, at the end of this road, we will understand how to live richly, but now, we have to walk that road regardless of how bumpy it might feel.

Do you remember the *Lord of the Rings* trilogy, when Sauron was defeated, the glory that Baggins and his adventurers experienced?[6] Or perhaps *Star Wars* and the joy the Jedi felt when the Dark Side and the Emperor were finally overcome?[7] Remember, there were many treacherous steps that led to that triumph. It was their collective persistence in the midst of adversity that inspires us. Those movies are reminiscent of our quest to walk together through the brokenness in order to see the glory at the end of the journey.

Pinning Blame

I know that there are some crazy and unfortunate circumstances, but our world is filled with stories of people choosing to make the most of a difficult situation.

In his iconic book, *Man's Search for Meaning*, Viktor Frankl tells us of his hellish three years in concentration camps during World War II. Frankl, a psychologist, was always looking to understand the reason why some individuals survived the awful conditions and others did not. His observation culminated in this statement: "Circumstances beyond our control can take everything from us in life except the freedom to choose how we will respond to those circumstances."[8]

Frankl gave great imagery of patients who held out for the hope of being home by Christmas. Yet when Christmas came and went with no promise of freedom, the death rate would rise substantially. His fellow prisoners died from a loss of hope. Additionally, Frankl saw that his decision to respond often enabled a higher authority to purpose his direction. He recalled certain instances where his decision to respond led his path to be divinely guided.

Responsibility: noun [9]

1. the state or fact of being responsible, answerable, or accountable for something within one's power, control, or management.

The natural response to challenging situations is to point blame in a certain direction. Blame is the opposite of responsibility, and another way for us to find our broken areas. Blame opens the doorway for anger to take root. When anger takes root, our excuses become relevant.

What or who do you blame? Is it true that you have responded to every situation that has crossed your path? Think about your responses and how they could have been different.

Healing Brokenness

Once we have discovered our brokenness, we can get on the road to healing. Although you probably don't want to hear it, that road begins with taking responsibility. Don't we collectively hate that word? It sounds like our parents lecturing us back in high school and college. However, within this theme of defining what it is we are seeking, I look at the root word, *response*. The question becomes, how do we respond to being broken?

My first real experience with being broke (and by broke, I mean having no money) came when I started my career in sales. I was full of ambition and desire. Liz and I had just gotten married, unwisely purchased a home, unfortunately relocated to a new "project," and were unaware of life on a commission-based income. These decisions were the writing on the wall. The funny thing is, during that time, we thought every decision was right. We had friends and family trying to encourage us in certain ways, but we stubbornly pursued our own agenda. Everything I thought I knew about the success I was after had vanished. It was one of the toughest days in my young professional career.

The hardest part of it all was knowing that small taste of financial freedom, only to have it yanked from my grasp. It would have been so much better if I had never tasted it at all. I was left dumbfounded as I faced our circumstances. *How had this all happened?*

Hindsight reveals significant foreshadowing of the decline, but at the time, I was too blind and stubborn to really see what was going on before me. It's incredibly difficult to be objective when your tastes have changed.

I remember the day I came home and sat in our guest

bedroom and cried, trying to hide from the truth. We didn't have enough money to pay our bills. The joy of buying our first house and new cars had crumbled to nothing more than debt and responsibility. The weight of those burdens was drowning me. My fear gave way to anger. I was mad at the world and mad at God. I blamed Him and everything else I could for the failure I was experiencing.

Why were people so shortsighted to stop buying luxury real estate? Why couldn't we generate the customers needed to sell more homes? *If they would just, if they would just, if they would just.* My *ifs* were the fingers I pointed at everything else. Somewhere in the middle of that anger, I heard the voice of truth:

If only you would have been more responsible.

At first, the thought made me incredibly angry, but then tears gave way to truth.

As I sobbed, I realized *I* was responsible for the condition we were in. Not the company, not the clients, not the market, and not God. Somewhere inside me, I knew that if I wanted to change, it was time to take responsibility. It was extremely difficult to accept. I knew that if I wanted things to change, I had to face the truth. *If you don't accept responsibility for where you are, how can you have any hope in being responsible for getting out of where you are?*

For Liz and me, the only way we would be able to survive financially was to sell the stock that Liz's grandfather left us when he died earlier that year. I wasn't sure how I was going to approach my wife with this request. She had been so gracious in going to work as well, adding her own financial contribution while completely supporting me emotionally the entire time.

When Liz walked in that night, she saw the look on my face and understood. She never hesitated and, amazingly, she wasn't even angry. Her spirit was calm as she made the phone call to sell her inheritance; it was just enough for us to make it through that month. Her grace and forgiveness spoke volumes to me.

Andy Andrews is my favorite author and a great resource of wisdom. His *New York Times* bestselling book *The Traveler's Gift* is a masterpiece. In it, he introduces the seven decisions for personal success, the first of which is taking responsibility. As he refers to it, *The Buck Stops Here*. Andy states:

> *If we don't accept responsibility for where we are right now, we have no hope of changing our future... We have the power to make choices that lead us to places we don't like. And that's great news! If we can make choices that lead us to places we don't like, then doesn't it stand to reason that we can also make choices that will lead us to a place we do like?*[10]

Man, that is so powerful, and it is exactly where I was as I sat on my bedroom floor sobbing. In the midst of my tears, I saw my own role in my circumstances. I had made some unwise decisions that had led me to that place. In hindsight, that was great news. If I had made bad choices that led me there, could different choices get me out? Most certainly they could.

For the majority of us, this is the most difficult part of the process; but again, it is the foundation for healing. If we see our brokenness as a condition that our circumstances have placed on us, we lie powerless. If brokenness is simply a condition that someone or something has placed upon you, how could you have any hope of changing it?

It is only when we understand our role in our brokenness that we gain the insight and the power to change. Taking responsibility is the first step to correctly healing your broken areas.

My experience healed a wound in my life that still reminds me today of certain things; most notably, how to manage money and how to make decisions. Had that experience not derailed the *Little Engine That Could,* I would have continued down the track of brokenness.

Assuming responsibility gives insight on how to manage future struggles. As adversity comes, you understand the power that you have to take responsibility. You gain clarity on how you will respond and you set yourself up for a better future.

Missing Forgiveness

When we face our past, we face two choices: to forgive or not to forgive. We can take Gary Weller's path, or we can remain in our bitter, crippled condition. One of the most powerful statements on this topic is,

Refusing forgiveness is like drinking poison and hoping the other person dies.

Failing to forgive and failing to ask for forgiveness where needed are chains on your heart that lead to an impoverished reality, far from the shores of richness.

Oddly enough, the more we choose not to forgive, the more control we give to our past. The more control we give to the people and circumstances we resent in the first place.

It's a crazy cycle that continues the spiral downward. Defining the word is a starting point for breaking that cycle.

Forgiveness: v. (the act of) [11]

1. to grant pardon for or remission of (an offense, debt, etc.);

2. to give up all claim on account of; remit

3. to grant pardon to (a person).

4. to cease to feel resentment against:

5. to cancel an indebtedness or liability

If you search the word *forgive*, you will find these definitions:

To grant pardon; to cease to feel resentment against

If you'll look closely, you'll notice both definitions start with an action; to grant and to cease. By definition, forgiveness is an action. I think we often fall into the trap of believing that forgiveness should be based on how we feel. It doesn't. To forgive is to simply make a decision, a choice, *regardless* of how you *feel*.

On my own journey, I needed Liz's forgiveness for the bad decisions I had made. When I saw her response and willingness to sell her inheritance, it gave me incredible confidence in her belief in us. Additionally, I needed to forgive myself. Rather than harbor frustration for my bad decisions, I needed to look at myself in the mirror, choosing to learn rather than be defeated.

As you journey through brokenness, be sure to check your emotions at the door. They will certainly be tested. However, you cannot let them defeat you. Abraham Lincoln once said, "I'm not concerned that you have fallen, I'm concerned that you arise!"

Being broken isn't about staying down. It's about healing. It's about rising. Most people fail to grasp the concept because all they can see is the brokenness. Remember, brokenness is the only condition that allows healing to take place.

Rise from the Ashes

Still having trouble with the idea that brokenness is necessary? Me too. It just hurts too badly sometimes. However, I ran across another natural occurrence that further cemented this truth.

Did you know that scientists and experts acknowledge that forest fires are an essential part of a forest ecosystem's life cycle? It seems ironic, doesn't it? In fact, some trees have seeds that won't sprout until their resin is burned. The process of the fire actually brings life. Additionally, the devastating fire removes dead trees, along with living ones, and returns rich nutrients to the soil. Read that again. The fire returns rich nutrients to the soil.

Similarly, have you ever come upon a fallen tree in the forest? When a tree falls in the forest and the decomposition begins, life abounds. Dead trees are teeming with life. They make a way for new life and they nourish the soil. Lastly, with the heavy foliage removed, sunlight can shine through and encourage growth. Heavy foliage often blocks light, a necessary part of growth, from reaching the surface.

What trees have grown in your life, obstructing the light you need for growth?

Dare I say, burn them down!

It's amazing to think that a fire is a necessary part of a healthy forest, but it's true. In the same sense, brokenness is necessary in your own life—an essential part of your growth. Understanding that truth and allowing its healing will correctly lead you down the right path. Look to your wounds, understand your brokenness, take responsibility, and choose forgiveness. By taking these actions, you refuse to be bound by your circumstances; instead, you rise above them.

Take a deep breath. I want you to remind yourself that you're not alone. The condition of brokenness is universal; no life is free from struggle. As I write this, I'm reminded of an old Bible story. The one of Adam and Eve in the Garden of Eden. What was once a kid's tale of people separated from their God has taken shape as a real-life truth.

Our lives reflect a separation from what we'd hope for. A distance between what we long for and where we are. Even with responsibility and forgiveness, there still seems to be something more. Take heart, knowing that you're not alone.

CHAPTER 7

Principle 2—Invest in Others

The Jackson Mawangi Story:
Helping Other People Everywhere

Deep in the plains of Nakuru, Kenya, there is a man seeking richness, despite living in one of the poorest environments imaginable. Jackson Mawangi, or Pastor Jackson to those who know him, is a native of Nakuru, Kenya. As pastor of the Victorious Gospel Church, he saw an epidemic in his area and he was overwhelmed with the conviction to do something about it. He saw an opportunity to invest.

Due to the rising violence in neighboring countries, Kenya is flooded with refugees, driving many to the streets. *Street children,* as they are referred to, live close to the garbage dump and often stay high by whatever means they can to escape their hunger and desperation, finding solace by sniffing glue and other hallucination-inducing substances. Because of this danger, these children are often beaten, abused, and on the run from the local authorities.

Pastor Jackson couldn't watch any longer. He felt called to act. In his own words, "The burden of this thing I wanted to do, helping the street orphans, was so strong." However, Jackson understood that he needed help. His resources and finances limited the execution of his vision; thus, he felt called to seek support from those he referred to as "his people." He didn't know where these people where, but he felt like God was leading him to the United States.

"In the midst of what I was doing, I was fully persuaded that I was doing exactly what I needed to be doing. With so many names and email addresses, I picked Port City Community Church."

Port City Church was a relatively new church in Wilmington, North Carolina, pastored by Mike Ashcraft. However, it was thousands of miles across a vast Atlantic Ocean. Jackson began an unlikely conversation with Mike about his vision for the street children. As Mike tells it, "I was getting ready for a sermon and I get a page from our receptionist. 'Mike, you have a call from Kenya.'" For two years the conversation between the pastors continued, albeit neither were fully aware of what was about to occur.

Despite his wife's full support, Jackson didn't have enough money for two tickets. His wife, known affectionately as Mama Hellen, said, "Go; obey God." Jackson responded, "I was feeling in my heart to sell our car and travel to USA to find someone who would help me to reach out to the street orphans and help them walk with God, so they can know they are a person and that He loves them."

Jackson sold his car and traveled to the airport in Nairobi some 150 miles away. He was devastated to realize his passport had expired; his journey was over. Confused, defeated, and feeling like he was in a trance, Jackson collapsed onto a bed at a local hotel in Nairobi.

All the while, his wife was praying he wouldn't return; that God would lead the way.

Jackson awoke the next morning with what he describes *as a peace to try again.* This time, he was graciously allowed to extend his passport, and he flew out of Nairobi, through London, and on to Baltimore, Maryland. While in Maryland, a local church hosted Jackson for two days and provided enough money for his bus ticket to Wilmington, North Carolina.

Jackson had been corresponding with Mike about his travels and two days later, he arrived. Looking back, nothing about this made sense to Mike. "Here we were, getting a call from this pastor in Kenya who says, 'You are my people.' It didn't make any sense, but I felt called to respond." Jackson had the opportunity to speak to the team at Port City, and they engaged a mission called HOPE 127; Helping Other People Everywhere.

Throughout the past seven years, the two have created an unlikely but impactful partnership to build Mama Hellen's Rehabilitation Center: a home complete with clean water and dormitories that provides hope for street children, numbering close to a hundred. In 2014, they opened an on-site primary school to provide much needed educational resources for these orphaned children.

To me, the most beautiful part of this story is that Jackson's vision of investing in others was made possible by the investment from others. Investment starts with an idea; nothing more, and nothing less. The amazing thing is that when an investment ignites the hearts of others, something special begins to evolve. It is a power that has created all of the world's largest charities and caregiving organizations. A simple idea grew. The growth of these ministries and the stories they pour out show us the power of investing. Evidence of this is apparent in my own life.

In 2010, my wife and I engaged with HOPE 127 through Port City Community Church. At the time, we really didn't know any details; we just simply responded to a call. We were told that our gift would be used to build a school and fund a ministry in Kenya. In turn, our family would sponsor one of the orphaned children. Having a child of our own that same year provided a unique opportunity for our family.

Three years ago, we began corresponding with Dennis Masaku, our sponsored child, through Port City's Kenya Project. Dennis was a thirteen-year-old orphan living at Mama Hellen's. Throughout these past three years, we have seen him grow in his love through his writing and in the pictures he sends us. We were to receive this letter from Dennis just this week:

> *How are you? I hope that you are fine and that the Lord is guiding you. Here in Mama Hellen's I am also doing very well in school. I am also working very hard in order to achieve good marks and also reach my dreams. My favorite memory verse is John 15:5:*

Jesus speaks, 'I am the vine; you are the branches. If you remain in me and I in you, you will bear much fruit; apart from me you can do nothing.'

I would also request you to read in the book of Proverbs 3:5-6 and you will be blessed. I hope that the Almighty God is guiding you. May you be blessed.

On the back of the handwritten letter, there is a carefully drawn heart with decorative letters reading:

I LOVE YOU VERY MUCH.

As I read this letter, my emotions poured out, flooding my heart. I was joyful. Joyful for Dennis and for the people who have been diligently carrying out the work to bring this ministry to life. I was heartbroken. Heartbroken for the millions of people across this world who are afflicted. Millions of people who think they don't matter. I was empowered. Empowered by the call to live our lives as a light unto the world. Empowered by a greater presence shaping our hearts.

In that moment, I learned about richness, hearing somewhere within that word a simple but impactful question:

Am I investing in others?

Investing doesn't only have to do with money; it can and should be your time as well. In the end, it has to do with your heart. My wife and I had been giving money to HOPE 127 for three years, but it wasn't until the week I received this letter that it really grabbed my heart.

I saw a beautiful, rich little boy in Nakuru, Kenya, taking the time to encourage me in every facet of my life. This time it wasn't about my investment each year—it was about Dennis's investment in my life.

Do you know what Proverbs 3:5–6 says?

Trust in the Lord with all your heart and lean not on your own understanding; in all your ways acknowledge Him and He will make your paths straight.

As I read that passage of Scripture, I began to understand that there was much more to the words *you make my life rich* than I could have ever imagined.

Understanding Your Investment

You may feel like your heart needs a reprieve. I understand. You feel like you're standing in a scorched forest wasteland and the sun is beating down on you. Hear this: you cannot walk this path alone; you will need something, or better yet, *someone*, to come alongside you and, in some cases, pick you up.

This brings us to the second principle in living richly:

I: *Invest in Others*

I wholeheartedly love this principle. People are my energy. I do understand that not everyone is wired as an extrovert, but that's not the point. The idea is to live a life that, in some way, pours over into others. The Jewish tradition has a practice where they place a large chalice in an even larger saucer. As they serve their wine into the chalice, it pours over into the saucer, reminding them of the concept of pouring into the lives of others.

Investing in others is an understanding that everyone has a story and every story matters. Too often our world tells us that it's all about us, but we often receive our greatest feeling of satisfaction and significance when we invest in others. Every person and every opportunity is uniquely different. Some people have a heart for certain stories, certain demographics. If you listen, your passion will tell you where you can invest. Wherever that is, seek the opportunities. The key is being open to listening to that call.

Invest: v. (used with object) [1]

1. to use, give, or devote (time, talent, etc.), as for a purpose;

2. to furnish or endow with a power, right, etc.; vest;

3. to endow with a quality or characteristic.

My world has been clouded with incessant noise, making it difficult for me to hear those whispers. That's why I intentionally believe that when we do hear them, we must respond. Investment opportunities are everywhere, not only in Kenya. They live right under your roof. In fact, that's where the investment starts every day. As a father to three boys and a husband, I need this question asked of me if I want any resemblance of richness in my life. Even Coach Weller told me that, in addition to understanding forgiveness and choosing to continue, the reason for his healing was largely attributed to the love and support of his wife Cathy and his countless friends.

Everyone has the ability to give of themselves, regardless of their financial positions. True richness is measured by the dividends of a life spent investing in others.

Ralph Waldo Emerson reminds us that the power is our own when he wrote the beautiful words, "We are rich only through what we give, and poor only through what we refuse."[2]

Still not convinced of the importance of investing? Let's look at it from a different angle.

Compound Me

Any financial advisor would agree that investing is a necessary part of building wealth. Investing is commonly defined *as putting money to use that can offer potential profitable returns*. However, with investing comes numerous strategies, rules, and opinions.

Essentially, it really isn't about what you have, but rather how you steward or manage what you are entrusted with. It reminds me of Jesus's Parable of the Talents.

As the story goes, a man entrusted three servants with various talents, or blessings, before he left on a journey. He planned to return but allowed his servants to steward his affairs while he was away.

To one he gave five talents, to another two, and to another, only one, each according to his ability. In his absence, these three servants handled their blessings in various ways. The one with five talents maximized his blessing and received five more for a total of ten. Likewise, the one with two talents was able to double his blessing. Lastly, the servant with one talent was fearful of losing his blessing, so he dug a hole and placed his talent in the ground.

When the master returned from his journey, he gathered his servants to give account for their actions. As the master saw that the first two men had been faithful with what they had been given, he spoke blessing upon them saying, "You have been faithful over a little; I will set you over much." However, the final servant, when called to give account for his actions, was ridiculed and ultimately thrown out of the master's presence because he had not been faithful with what he had been given.

Now I'm no pastor, but I do know that everyone has been entrusted with different talents, gifts, and abilities. Too often we catch ourselves sitting around grumbling about the talents, gifts, and abilities we didn't get rather than taking advantage of the opportunity to use what we've been given to our greatest potential. Even with very little, there is the opportunity for compounding. In the end, this parable teaches us that if we are faithful with little, opportunities will be provided for us to be faithful with much more. This is the principle of compounding.

The most notable financial tool is the concept of compound interest: interest earned on interest earned. I'm sure you've heard, "Save early and save often." These words are meant to guide you to take advantage of the great benefit of compound interest.

Investopedia.com defines compound interest as:

> *Interest that accrues on the initial principal and the accumulated interest. Compounding interest allows a principal amount to grow at a faster rate than simple interest which is calculated as a percentage of only the principal amount.*[3]

Once you take the step to begin, your investment starts to grow upon itself. Interestingly enough, in our quest for personal richness, investing is equally essential. However, the investment you should seek is in the lives of others. I like to think of it like this: investing in people yields compound opportunity—opportunity for growth, opportunity for wisdom, and opportunity to become the person you were created to be. As we give, we transcend as we become part of a bigger story. It stands to reason that, without others, we fail to live richly because we fail to be provided opportunity. More importantly, recognizing the difference in others' lives gives us power to live beyond ourselves.

In 1624, English poet John Donne penned these words: "No man is an island, entire of itself."[4] These words hold true nearly four hundred years later because they are. We live in a beautifully interconnected world where our actions affect those around us. We can't ignore this. The decisions you make and the actions you take send ripples throughout lives, though many people never slow down to notice.

I received an email from a friend a few weeks ago thanking me for actions I took in high school, almost fifteen years prior. I never had any idea that the often immature actions of my seventeen-year-old self would have impacted someone else, but they did. Do you know what it taught me? People are watching. And I'm not just talking about myself; I'm talking about all of us. People are watching you, waiting to be encouraged. People are longing for you to invest in them, even when you don't feel like it.

We must embrace not only our ability, but our calling to invest in others. This doesn't come from a feeling, but rather from a responsibility. The beautiful part I'm beginning to understand is that this type of investing yields returns for life. As Maya Angelou said, "Giving liberates the soul of the giver."[5] In other words, the soul of the one investing is the one who is made rich. If you're feeling especially poor, the first place I'd ask you to look is how you are helping and being helped by others. If you remove others, you remove richness.

Simple Daily Practices

I want to reiterate that, while I do think we are all interconnected and international investment is important, we cannot ignore the opportunities right before us. The truth is, we encounter people daily. The easy response is to shut off and shut up, hoping we won't have to engage. We're so guilty of this, aren't we? If our opportunities come from people, why would we do this? I toe this line with believing that we either think we don't matter or we think other people don't care. Yet, both of those couldn't be further from the truth. We know we matter because people matter to us, and we know people care because we've seen someone light up before us after the slightest investment of a compliment. If both of those assumptions aren't true, we can't ignore the opportunity. Countless opportunities to invest in others cross our paths daily. Everywhere we go, everyone we encounter needs encouragement.

One of the simplest practices I can think of is calling people by name. The technological age we live in creates a chasm between person-to-person interactions. With Facebook and Twitter, who needs to be face-to-face? That line of thinking seems to run rampant, driving us further into our corners. I noticed this when I started connecting with different groups on social media sites. These groups were brought together based on common interests, but in every one, I could see that people longed for actual person-to-person interaction. My theory proved right as I began to notice countless conversations about meet-ups. As the members of the group would travel, they would throw out an opportunity to meet up with the other group members in that area. Folks were exchanging tweets to meet in airports, hotel lobbies, and restaurants as a way to engage the much-needed, face-to-face interaction.

Since you don't always have the opportunity to travel and meet up with your social circles, it becomes increasingly important to interact with those you do encounter. The waiter at lunch, the barista serving you coffee, the cashier at the grocery store all have one thing in common, a name. The easiest way to interact with folks in that situation is to call them by their names. If they don't happen to have a name tag on, simply ask them and I promise they'll tell you.

I have a great friend named Larry who is the champion of calling folks by name. I mean he *always* calls people by their names. I love eating lunch with him, especially at a restaurant he frequents. It is amazing to watch every server come up and speak to him, and not just the one waiting on him that day. The other servers will go out of their way to say hello. I promise you this: Larry is never in need of a condiment or a refill. He gets the best service of anyone I've ever eaten with. Every time I eat lunch with Larry, I feel like I'm eating with Elvis reincarnated. He encourages me by this simple action, and his life reflects blessings as he invests in others.

Investing in others is about engaging your surroundings, becoming aware of things that would be easily overlooked if your eyes were on yourself, and taking the initiative to be in each moment. Asking your servers their names may sound too ordinary, but they will have a profound impact on you. Especially when you start practicing this at places you frequent.

Personally, I know that Colleen, Lauri, Tom, and Janet serve me at Panera. Jackie, Erin, Deb, and Jen at Starbucks. Think about it: most of the places you tend to frequent are the places where you've begun to know people by their names. That personal interaction adds the element of relationship to any transaction. Once you've created a first-name basis, you'll see that these small relationships begin to build a foundation of trust. From there, you won't be able to contain the stories.

The morning of September 11, 2013, I found myself at my usual Starbucks, grabbing a venti Pike Place to start the day. I normally make my coffee at home, but this particular morning, I decided to engage my surroundings. For most Americans, that day weighs heavy on our hearts and spirits. Facebook becomes flooded with iconic American symbols and sayings as we remember the tragedy of the towers' fall and the rise of the American spirit.

As I was in line, I overheard someone mention, "Be sure to thank Jen today. Remember she served NYPD twelve years ago."

Immediately I saw it in Jen's eyes. She had been there. She had witnessed everything firsthand. I didn't know her personally beyond our hellos, but I saw her story in her eyes. It rushed over me, all that she had to have witnessed on that fateful day. Yet, it touched me because here she was, still serving. Instead of the citizens of New York, she was serving me. Yes, it was only coffee, but she still served.

This moved my soul, and I wrote about Jen on my blog that day. I wrote about how important it was to tell these stories. Stories keep the spirit alive. Stories tell of the rise after the fall. Jen's story encouraged me.

A couple of months later, completely out of the blue, Jen pulled me aside to thank me for sharing her story. She showed me where she had saved it in her phone and she told me that she would, on occasion, take a look. She also told me that she had called her mom and shared with her. Over the next few months, Jen and I began a friendship because of I used her name and engaged in simple conversations. Jen told me about her three kids and how her husband had a difficult time finding a job, so she went back to work as a barista at Starbucks to help her family.

It wasn't a fancy, name-in-lights moment, but hopefully it showed Jen that she was appreciated. Hopefully it showed her that she mattered. She mattered to me.

She bought my coffee that day despite my trying to argue otherwise. I wouldn't tell her boss, but from then on, she never let me pay for coffee.

Giving liberates the soul of the giver.

The Purpose of Giving

There is a dichotomy here I want to unveil.

The cynic in you says, *You're only investing because you're trying to leverage other people. You're doing it for your own benefit.*

This is the idea that you use generosity to gain power and control. While this is unfortunately a motive for some, it is not what we're looking for. This fault is the vice of investing that is driven by greed and power. Don't fall into this trap. While investing in others will provide you opportunity, you don't do it for that reason. You do it because it brings you your greatest joy.

Eleanor Roosevelt said it like this, "Since you get more joy out of giving joy to others, you should put a good deal of thought into the happiness that you are able to give."[6]

I'm reminded of the classic Charles Dickens tale, *A*

Christmas Carol. I prefer the Disney version myself, *Mickey's Christmas Carol*, where Ebenezer Scrooge is Scrooge McDuck. Regardless, you know the tale: Scrooge leveraged people for the impact it had, not on his life, but on his wallet. If you remember anything about Scrooge, remember that once he had a vision from the ghosts of Christmas Past, Present, and Future, he left miserable. Keep taking, hoarding, and leveraging people, and you'll be miserable too. The moral of Dickens's story: don't be a Scrooge; it cripples the soul!

Generosity: n., plural generosities. [7]

1. readiness in giving.

2. freedom from meanness or smallness of mind or character.

Now, I need to emphasize here that although Dickens's story highlights Scrooge's wealth, it is not the money that mattered. The financial component has no bearing on your ability to give, but even more so when you do. Think of the blessing that Scrooge was once he started using his money as a way to bless those around him. True investing has far more to do with your heart than with your wallet.

In his second letter to the church at Corinth, the Apostle Paul puts it best when he says,

> *You will be made rich in every way so that you can be generous on every occasion, and through us your generosity will result in thanksgiving to God. (2 Corinthians 9:11)*

Paul knew of a greater purpose for our richness. That it would spark generosity, and that generosity, would lead to thanksgiving to God.

The Gift of Recognition

A great way to invest with your heart is to embrace the opportunity of recognition. Nothing feels better than being recognized, does it? Who doesn't love getting a handwritten letter in the mail? Who doesn't love praise from his boss? Who doesn't love it when her spouse does something special to say *thank you?* If we're honest, we all do. However, we often fall into the trap of letting these special moments slip away.

Robert D. Smith in his book *20,000 Days and Counting* gives us a crash course on mastering our lives today. He talks about the importance of focusing on today and encourages questions as we embark. He proposes seven questions for every single day that create a passion and a purpose for our lives. His first question:

Whose life am I going to brighten today?[8]

What an incredible question to ask yourself when you wake up each morning. What would happen if you set yourself on fire to brighten the lives of others?

Smith calls this the gift of a standing ovation. When we watch our favorite team or hear a great speaker, we stand and cheer. However, in our daily lives, people are always adding some benefit to us, yet we rarely acknowledge it. Robert embraces it as his job to give outstanding ovations as if his favorite team were in the Super Bowl.

Give people around you standing ovations for their impact in your life, regardless of how big or small. Whether it's the server at the restaurant or the person pouring your coffee, someone is helping you today. How can you thank them? More importantly, someone around you is going through a difficult time. What can you do for them?

When you start molding your heart to seek investment in others, opportunities will abound. The garbage man, your unruly neighbor, that annoying coworker—all of them are longing for the investment from someone. Why not you? You will be blessed beyond measure if you start pouring into the lives of others. And the greatest part of all? You have no idea the power it holds.

Could You Imagine?

Our sponsored child, Dennis Masaku, aspires to go to college. He has written to us that this is his greatest dream along with becoming a pilot. Follow me down this hypothetical rabbit trail.

Dennis enters the University of Nairobi after his graduation from the orphanage and primary school. After his four years there, he graduates with a degree in mechanical engineering and enlists in flight school. After a few years, he secures his license to become a helicopter pilot, responsible for the transport of those in dire need.

Years down the road, one of my sons has decided to go into the mission field and has been placed in Kenya to assist with the continuation of the primary school at Mama Hellen's. While repainting the orphanage, my son falls from his ladder, traumatically injuring his spine. He's in need of an airlift. Could it be possible that the same family who invested in Dennis's childhood would be in need of an airlift after a devastating accident? Could it be possible that Dennis would have the blessing of returning the favor? It absolutely could! Picture this in your mind; let it move in your soul! Embrace the opportunity you have to invest in others; you never know the dividends it may pay. It may not manifest itself in this fashion, but you never know, so keep investing. The returns will pay dividends for life.

Two Quick Tips

There are two distinctive actions I try to employ every day to remind me to invest in everyone I encounter.

1. Holding Doors—I can hear those of you who aren't from the South saying, "Yeah, yeah..." Hear me out on this. I have found that by making the simple effort to hold a door for someone takes an encounter into something deeper, a place below the surface. In a world so full of noise and busyness, taking a few seconds to grab the door for someone is your free investment in that moment.

Two years ago, I started walking my clients to the door after our appointments. In my mind, it showed appreciation and my way of saying, "Thank you; you matter." People were so appreciative that now, I run ahead of them just to hold the door. In all honesty, I started getting comments from others in my office. Before I knew it, I started noticing that others were doing the exact same thing. I'll let you guess how it affected sales. Our office went on to win the Honor Agency as one of the top in our state. Now I'm not suggesting it was all from simply holding the door for our clients, but we began a culture of appreciation through the smallest token of investment.

On the flip side, there are the people who don't acknowledge when you hold the door for them, as if they expected it. As a hilarious social experiment, I want to follow those folks around all day holding doors for them. I'm curious to see how many times it takes for them to notice. Give this simple practice a shot, and I promise it will return tenfold.

2. Smiling—Yep, it's that simple. Try smiling more. Some of our scowls are downright scary. In my mind, putting on a smile is like dressing up in a tuxedo. Who doesn't look good in a tuxedo, right? Smile at people you meet, smile at your co-workers, smile at your spouse, smile at your kids; for goodness sakes, *smile!* Smiles cost nothing and are among the greatest gifts you can give.

I recently had the opportunity to talk to a group of soon-to-be college graduates and I could feel the heaviness of responsibility weighing on them as they faced their futures. The pressure of getting a job and considering a career loomed ominously over them. As we discussed these principles, I offered them this suggestion with a promise that they would land jobs. I could see the puzzled looks on their faces, but as I brought this to life, they started recognizing that all of their friends who had recently been hired were some of the most smiling people they knew! It was so awesome to see their recognition of the effects of this simple gesture come to life.

3. I Know I Said Two, but... Combine 1 and 2 and *look out!* If you hold doors *and* smile at people, you might as well have put peanuts in M&Ms—greatest combination ever!

Seeking Others' Investment

The flip side of this principle is seeking the investment of others.

This isn't a desperate cry for help, and it's not begging for investment. There is a fine line between someone who seeks help and someone who asks for it. Never be afraid to ask for help if you need it, but seeking it is slightly different. Seeking has an active component to it. Someone who is seeking is actively searching.

The first part is simple geography. Align yourself with who drive you toward richness. If you long for the waters of wisdom, build your house close to their shores. The question then becomes, who are you spending time with?

My grandfather had a saying, *If you lie down with dogs, you'll get up with fleas.* Parents are always concerned about their kids' friends. Don't you remember growing up? If you're a parent, aren't you terribly concerned about that now? I've had conversation after conversation with folks who just can't seem to get out of a rut. After a quick look at their friends, I totally understand. I don't intend to sound judgmental with this, but choose wisely who you're around. The truth is, you're always being influenced by others, so choose them with care.

I'm sure you know grumpy people who complain about everything under the sun. I really hope you're not that person! If you aren't, but are surrounded by them, watch out; you may just become them. However, if you already feel like the negative grump, that's great because knowing is the first step. There's a common reference to this type of people. We call them Eeyores. Be cautious of the Eeyores of the world.

On lifehack.com, Dustin Wax wrote a great article about not being an Eeyore:

> *One of the barriers to a happy, effective life is the way that we create negativity in our daily affairs. We swap stories of adversity as a way of passing time, of connecting with each other.*[9]

It's important to know what Eeyores look like so we can avoid them. Eeyores look for problems rather than solutions; in fact, Eeyores *create* problems where none exist. One of the best ways I've heard it said is, "The part of your mind that you feed is the part of your mind that grows." If you're constantly feeding yourself with negativity, you can't help but see negativity grow within you.

If you had the choice, wouldn't you rather be around someone who lifts your spirit; someone who is positive and joyful? We absolutely would because joy is contagious. You laugh around other people who laugh and you smile around those who smile; you can't help but to do so.

Observing the characteristics in those we are around makes us aware of our own characteristics as well. Start gravitating toward people you aspire to be like. Understand how they act, how they treat others, as a way to mirror those actions in your own life.

So what is a friend?

Friends come in all shapes and sizes with varying familiarity. Some you talk to daily, while others carry on a conversation for years, actually only seeing each other occasionally. And, like the seasons, friends come and go. Whether by death or distance or circumstance, these folks are in our lives for a time, only to fade into the memories of tomorrow. However, there's one characteristic of friendship I've come to cherish.

Friends help us *get our wings*. Within a friendship is a mutual idea of help that is unique to those involved. The common notion of a friend who is all-accepting seems to be very dangerous ground. This is because someone who accepts you as you are doesn't help much at all. Quite frankly, they really don't care. To me, friendship is much more. A friend engages. A friend invests. A friend challenges. A friend cares.

They stand alongside us when needed, yet they'll run out ahead of us to blaze a trail. They don't have to share our journeys or our passions, yet they care enough to ask. When we talk, they listen. And, should they see us off the track they know we'd hope to be on, they'll meet us where we are, yet forbid themselves to leave us there. Friends hold up pictures of who we'd hope to become and mirrors to show us who we really are. I hope to continually learn what it means to become a better friend.

And, this doesn't mean you have to physically be around them all the time. Associate your Twitter feed, your Facebook feed, your iPod selections to things that move you in the direction you want to go. Rich people hang around rich people.

To See What's Going On, Understand What's Going In

Are you familiar with the phrase, "Garbage in, garbage out"? This adage derives itself from early computer software struggles. As reviews of computer output were conducted, testers realized the wrong answers were being produced. After much research and study, figures inputted wrongly were discovered to be the issue. Imagine that! If we pour useless, negative energy into our lives, it stands to reason that meaningful, positive energy will not flow out of our lives.

Studies everywhere document the countless hours of television people watch. I won't specify those numbers, but I think this is a common plague affecting our culture. I'm always amazed to hear singles question why their relationships aren't working when their relationship diets are fueled by reality dating shows. It stands to reason, if you want advice on dating or if you desire a beneficial outcome, surround yourself with people who have great marriages. Most reality shows fuel themselves on the one thing most hated in relationships: drama.

Rather, as you observe desirable characteristics of successful relationships, you'll develop a clearer vision of what you desire in your own relationships. On the contrary, wallowing in the pit of despair with others who are stuck there themselves is insanity. Your words become a proverbial shovel, digging you deeper into a hole. Instead, seek those who will throw you a line and pull you out.

Filling Your Time

The one common factor of all people is time. Each of us have twenty-four hours in every day; no more, no less. Therefore, time is a cheap excuse for those who simply don't want to change.

Your time is precious, and you can never replenish it. We all know that. However, we fall into a trap of believing that we can't choose how to spend it. Numerous people ask me, "How do you have the time?" The answer is simple. Countless, inefficient seconds add up to minutes and hours. Better stated, these precious lost moments are better spent investing in the future.

Think about your morning while you get ready for the day. Think about your commute to work. Think about walking your dog. What are you doing in these moments? Your efficiency is limited if you're not using those times seeking investment. Of course, sometimes you need to shut off the noise and enjoy some peace and quiet. You need time to reflect and rest. But all too often, we are very inefficient with our time.

I once asked a mentor how he found time to read. His response was very simple, "I have someone read to me." This puzzled me at first, but I quickly realized he was referring to audio books. With so much technology at our fingertips, we ought to utilize the opportunity to be read to. Podcasts and audiobooks are my personal favorites, and I can enjoy them almost anywhere.

Michael Hyatt, *New York Times* bestselling author of *Platform*, talks about his routine in reading new material . Michael is a runner and sets aside time each week to listen to audio books as he runs. At this pace, Michael is able to listen to roughly one book per week. That's fifty new books a year. Can you imagine the nuggets of investment that are being poured into his life? Michael is considered the expert on intentional leadership, yet he's *still* seeking investment. Additionally, his schedule is as demanding as anyone's. If he can find time, then so can we.

In 2010, I took up the sport of triathlon. I certainly wasn't a triathlete. Team sports had always been my forte: baseball, basketball, and football. Having grown up at the beach, I had swum before, but just playfully, never as an athlete. I had ridden a beach cruiser; did that count?

A few years removed from college and the enjoyment of a desk job left me out of shape and in need of motivation. Adult league softball wasn't cutting it. I was mad that I had regressed so much from my high school and college years. I was a shadow of my former, athletic self, if there ever was such a thing. When I learned that we were expecting our first child, I saw the need for change. I didn't want to live a life that led my son to ever accept complacency. I wanted to be in my midforties and still keeping up with the physical prowess of a teenager.

So, the sport of triathlon became my passion. During my in-season training sessions, I spend a lot of hours cycling and running. At the time, I found that this conflicted with my reading and writing. That was until I found out about an indoor trainer. An indoor trainer allows you to fix the back wheel of a bicycle, getting a full workout while remaining stationary. It allowed me to read while I was riding, making my time highly effective. This is just a simple example of bundling your time to make it the most effective. If reading is important, you have to find a way to make that investment in your life. I think Dr. Seuss said it best, "The more that you read, the more things you will know. The more that you learn, the more places you'll go."[10]

Investing for the Future Harvest

In the end, we must not neglect the absolute power of investing in others. Martin Luther King, Jr. said, "Life's most persistent and urgent question is, 'What are you doing for others?'"[11]

If you're not asking yourself this question, your life will fall short of everything you hoped it would be. In turn, if you are asking yourself this question and seeking opportunities to invest in others, your life will begin to take shape. You'll find richness at your fingertips. Your heart will experience change.

How we invest in others helps us shape what we believe about ourselves. Once we invest, we start to see the good in us, and it is empowering. As the farmer works the soil of his field, readying it for the planting of seeds, so must our souls prepare for a future harvest. Working in the lives of others is simply plowing the fields of our hearts, getting them ready. Remember the forest fire? Brokenness allows the richness to return to the soil. Investing in others tills the soil, making it ready for the seeds. What seeds, you ask? In your journey to redefine richness, you are now ready for the seeds of gratitude.

CHAPTER 8

Principle 3—Choose Gratitude

The Peyton Fontenot Story:
Truly Grateful

Life is full of challenges, some greater than others. How we respond to those challenges shapes our journeys.

On May 15, 2006, Ron and Sarah Fontenot welcomed their sweet baby girl, Peyton Elisabeth, into this world. Having a history of serious pregnancy and postpartum complications, Sarah was monitored very closely throughout her entire thirty-seven-week pregnancy.

Everything looked much better this time around. The only hiccup was a thirty-six-week ultrasound that showed a larger-than-normal spacing between the back of Peyton's brain and her skull. There was no real cause for alarm, but they knew she'd have an ultrasound after she was born.

No worries. Not yet.

On May 15th, Sarah was induced, and Peyton came into this world crying, looking as perfect as any baby imaginable.

The following day, following Peyton's ultrasound, Sarah and Ron were shocked to the core to learn something was wrong with their baby girl.

The ultrasound confirmed the abnormal spacing. By the end of the day on May 16th, Peyton had a list of medical complications that had everyone concerned for her life. The pediatrician noted cataracts, hip dysplasia, a heart murmur, and hearing loss. She was also missing a portion of the back of her brain. Within two weeks' time, she had two separate surgeries and on top of all of her issues, Sarah was back in the hospital with a massive pulmonary embolism—a life-threatening blood clot.

Sarah had little time for recovery as she jumped into life with a new baby, much less one with multiple medical complications. Additionally, their older daughter, Moira, needed love and attention of her own.

Sarah and Ron were both working full-time jobs and felt ill-equipped to handle everything Peyton struggled with. By her first birthday, she had endured eight surgeries. With no outside help, they were desperately aware that they were burning the candle at both ends at an ever-increasing and exhausting pace. They utilized all the resources they could to help Peyton with her complex situation, but it still wasn't enough.

They were barely functioning, and something needed to give, fast.

So, Ron and Sarah made one of the biggest decisions of their married life. Although they were not in a financial position to take the step, Sarah quit her job to stay home with their daughters. The choice was vital to the life of their family. Shortly thereafter came the decision to uproot their family and move from Texas to South Carolina when Ron received a more lucrative job opportunity. When they took this leap of faith in the summer of 2008, they had no idea what that meant, as they were not particularly rooted in faith. They were rooted in their lives and the responsibility to their family situation; they were always busy in the day-to-day.

They were casual churchgoers and, if anything, growing farther and farther away from what little faith they had. To them, faith was denominational religion, a ceremonial practice having little to do with personal feeling or relationship. After making the big move to South Carolina, they couldn't find a church that was a good fit with their customary practices, and one particularly awful experience nearly drove them away from church altogether.

That was until a friend reached out in 2009. Acknowledging their desperate need for something, they reached back. In the process, they discovered something deeper: they were reaching out to God. And that was the turning point.

A single-income life allowed them to breathe as the stress of an outside job was no longer a hindrance. In spite of that relief, Sarah was still tired. Her physical and mental resources were stretched to the breaking point. In her own words, she explained, "While I never blamed God for the situation we were in, I would not have said that I believed He was doing a great work through it."

Their faith was growing but had no focus.

Sarah continued, "Looking back on our lives since that point, I can see that the decision to go to church changed the course of our lives. I'm so grateful for the invitation from our friend. We still call that church our home today. In essence, if it weren't for Peyton, we wouldn't know God. Of that, I am certain. If it weren't for her, we wouldn't have faced the decision for me to quit working outside of the home. If it weren't for her, we wouldn't have wound up moving across the country in search of a better life as a family. If it weren't for her, we would never have been led to our church. Without that, we wouldn't know God."

What started as an incredible responsibility with never-ending questions began to turn into a blessing. Still, in the years that followed, Peyton's life became increasingly complex.

New medical challenges arose constantly, and home nursing became necessary. Although helpful, it wasn't the nurses' responsibility to raise Peyton. It wasn't their responsibility to be her parent. The nurses loved Peyton, but she wasn't theirs. Ron and Sarah were the only ones who could deal with the heartbreak that came with knowing their daughter would never develop past a nine-month mental capacity. She would never walk, talk, sit, stand, or crawl.

Despite those difficult realizations, Sarah started to see something.

"As we began our journey with God, I started to learn a difficult truth. In order for me to fully accept what was happening with Peyton, I needed to change my heart. I needed to start being thankful. I was constantly reminded of a verse shared with us by our new church family:

Be thankful in all circumstances, for this is God's will for you who belong to Christ Jesus. (1 Thessalonians 5:18)

In a world where that language seems cliché and overused, it started to make incredible sense to Sarah. *Be thankful.* As their journey continued, they learned to be thankful in *all* situations.

Peyton would have a total of twenty surgeries and countless more emergency room visits. Each time the easy answer was to throw in the towel. However, they learned that if they could just give thanks for a few things each day, it completely changed their outlook. It didn't matter how big or small those things were; they just needed to find something, *anything*, to be thankful for. A chance for a change in perspective. Perspective that would be essential as the only sustainer of hope during their most difficult time.

On May 4, 2013, their journey with Peyton on this earth would come to an end, just eleven days before her seventh birthday. She passed away at sunrise that morning. A grief they had never known washed over Ron and Sarah for the loss of their precious child. Yet, somewhere within, they gave thanks to God.

Sarah explained, "I am thankful for being entrusted with the life of such a special gift from God. She was His perfect creation on loan to us for a brief period. Our grief is strong, and we mourn this loss each day, but God equipped me for a challenge that I did not feel equipped at all to face. He provided the strength to rise to the daily challenges of life on this seven-year journey. Even in the darkest moments when we faced the decisions that no parent should have to make, I know that God was there with us. He never left us once. I didn't recognize Him at work back in 2006, but were it not for Peyton's life, I would never have come to know Him at all. I am thankful to have been richly blessed by this sweet little girl."

When I met Sarah in early 2014, I was moved by her story. As soon we began talking, I knew there was purpose to the crossing of our paths. At that time, I asked Sarah if she would be willing to share parts of Peyton's story and their journey on my blog. She and Ron graciously obliged.

What happened next moved us all.

The day Peyton's story ran on my blog, Sarah received a call from Boston Children's Hospital. This was the hospital in charge of numerous tests to determine Peyton's unknown condition. For months, even years, Sarah and Ron had longed to know what they were really dealing with, but no doctors were able to tell them. That was, until now.

Peyton suffered from a very rare genetic condition, one that was not documented in any other medical literature they could find. A rare chromosomal disorder in Peyton's genetic makeup prohibited her body from processing copper, causing a chain reaction that led to her many ailments. When doctors tested Ron and Sarah, they learned a very unique thing. Each of them held a silent version of the rare condition that was only made active in Peyton's life.

A life that would be lived for only seven years. Seven years that would teach Ron and Sarah so much more than they could ever teach their daughter. In such a very short time, Peyton's life impacted so many. As Sarah closed our time together, she shared something greatly meaningful.

"In hindsight, the timing was perfect. God blessed us with Peyton's perfect timing because He knew it would take seven years for His purpose to be fulfilled. I am grateful to have known her and to have been a part of her life. I am grateful to God for opening my heart to Him to do His will. It is through Him that we were equipped. It took two imperfect people and one perfect God to create a perfect little girl who would radiate His truth into our lives."

Peyton Fontenot taught us about richness far beyond that of any financial measure, a richness from above. A richness found through gratitude.

Choose Gratitude

Peyton's story is the perfect culmination of understanding brokenness and investing in others. It brings us right to where we are. We have burned down our forest and wrestled with our brokenness. We have taken responsibility; we have embraced forgiveness; we are beginning to heal. We have begun investing in others and have seen the dividends doing so pays.

We are here. Our soil is ready.

> **Gratitude**: noun [1]
> 1. the quality or feeling of being grateful or thankful; warmly or deeply appreciative of kindness or benefits received

In our lives, our soil is our soul, the deepest part of us. That part often buried inside that calls to us as we read stories like those of Coach Weller, Pastor Jackson, and Peyton. It is there where true richness begins. In the process of living richly, the soil of our soul must be ready for the seeds of gratitude.

The third principle to redefine the meaning of rich is:

C: *Choose Gratitude*

All too often, the world tells us that gratitude is circumstantial; it is a by-product of our environment. I believe differently. Gratitude is a choice we must learn to make should we want to live the true life awaiting us. I like to think of gratitude as the currency of living richly. It is the exchange by which we enjoy and experience life to the fullest. As we earn money, we must learn gratitude. Choose gratitude.

Gratitude often seems fleeting and circumstantial. For most, if it's hot outside, they're hot; and if it's cold outside, they're cold. In regard to gratitude, if things are good, we're grateful. But forget it if things aren't going our way.

On this journey, we must understand how to be grateful regardless of our circumstances. We must choose it above all else. If we can seek gratitude as our foundational response, we are secure to build upon it. Otherwise, we crumble amid our circumstances.

A Deeper Meaning

Mike Ashcraft and Rachel Olsen co-authored a great book that helps us realize the power of our words and the failure of our resolutions—*My One Word*.

After failing year after year at keeping New Year's resolutions, Mike created the My One Word concept. The idea is to focus your energy and attention on one word as you walk through your year. As he says, "Change is possible, but focus is required."[2] It's not about swearing off your past; it's about focusing on what you are becoming. Therefore, your resolution doesn't become a checklist; it becomes a process to focus on daily.

I've been walking in this practice for about five years now; picking a word and using it as the lens to move toward my future. As I began writing this book, I never knew how impactful my word was going to be to the work at hand.

I knew the concept of gratitude was something I wanted to grab hold of, but I felt like something was missing. As I searched for a better understanding of the word *grateful*, I wrote it down and stared at it for a minute.

GRATEFUL

Then, I let the word come to life as I spelled it like this:

GREATFULL

I stared at it again, slowly absorbing its meaning. Having perspective and understanding the concept of gratitude leads to greatness. It leads to richness. To make life rich is to fully understand the choice to be grateful.

I know I cheated a little bit and combined two words, but that's the beauty of the process. It sparks creativity and clarity as you dig in. I grabbed ahold of that word, *greatfull*, and at that moment, it became a beacon of hope in my life. *Greatfull* was My One Word. Every day as I met challenges, I was reminded of gratitude and the greatness that was waiting, should I only choose its path.

Pursuing greatness through the lens of gratitude.

I became intentionally thankful for everything, even the common inconveniences of head colds, flu bugs, and disrupted plans. I started reading and listening to things that taught me about gratitude; filling my mind and heart with influences that pushed me toward my word. Podcasts on gratitude. Books on perspective. Conversations about dreaming. Gratitude began to take root in my heart, and it began to grow fruit. It became active, initiating a pursuit of greatness. It wasn't always constant, but I began to notice old habits and tendencies when I wasn't focused on gratitude. My heart, now inclined toward gratitude, began to reject everything else.

The misspelling helps me understand that it is only through being grateful that I can grow. It grants me clarity as I live out every day.

Had I started the year with a list of resolutions that looked like this:

- Focus on my walk with Christ
- Become a better husband
- Become a better father
- Grow my business
- Run a half marathon
- Start a blog
- Write a book
- Build a new home

I would have likely failed. Twelve months later, I now know, "Change is possible, focus is required." I highly encourage you to visit the concept of My One Word as well.

So where does gratitude begin and how can we focus on it? In my discovery, I ran across an old favorite story.

Gratitude Defined: A Heart Issue

Gratitude is defined as:

Thankful; being deeply appreciative of benefits received.

It comes from the Latin word *gratus*, as does the word *grace*. *Grace*, on the other hand, is defined as:

Favor or goodwill.

Something unique happens when those two definitions merge.

When we do this, we find that the purpose of gratitude is to see favor and goodwill, even in the most difficult scenarios. While one man may look at the rain as dampening his day, another sees it as a blessing for his crops. Our ability to see favor and goodwill is completely contingent upon our perspective. Therefore, gratitude becomes a shift in perspective. A choice to see things differently. Essentially, gratitude is simply a way of thinking. You're either grateful or ungrateful. Much like forgiveness, it is a choice we make.

Gratitude is imperative because it engages us in the moment, forcing us to make a choice. Ingratitude binds us to bitterness and anger, removing us from the moment. This downward spiral leads to a callousness that cannot yield healthy fruit. If we want a beneficial foundation for growth, we must choose gratitude and engage in life.

A great rebirth is happening in pop culture today: the rebirth of 3D. I remember the cheap, plastic glasses with one red lens and one blue of my childhood that allowed *Jaws* to dive off of the screen and into the audience. Actually, I still have trouble swimming in salt water because of it. 3D video technology is effective because it allows our perspective to change. It engages us in the action.

Engaging gratitude is like putting on those cheap, black frames. It draws you in to the story. You become a participant in the action. If you see through a lens of gratitude, things begin to jump out at you.

You can see beauty and purpose in polar opposites, such as the tranquility of an early morning or the cry of a newborn, the gentleness of a breeze or the ferocity of a storm. Every situation allows you the opportunity to be grateful; it just depends on your perspective. Consider your perspective and choose gratitude.

Greatness is difficult to deny, particularly in athletics. Each sport has its own great, its own champion. In 1973, the world saw greatness as never before.

Regardless of your knowledge of horse racing, you've certainly heard of Secretariat. *Big Red*, as he was called, was the greatest thoroughbred horse of all time, winning the Triple Crown in 1973. I have always been in awe of this horse and what he was able to accomplish. The special fact about Secretariat that completely astounds me is that he still holds the track records at *all three* Triple Crown races.

Yet, it was after his death when his legend grew. That's when his story became even more interesting.

Upon his death in 1989, a necropsy revealed something amazing. Secretariat's heart, his engine, was almost three times the size of a normal horse's heart. It weighed an estimated twenty-two pounds! In horse racing, this genetic condition is referred to as the "X-Factor" and many great Thoroughbreds have the same condition. In fact, Secretariat's biggest competitor, Sham, had it too. Sham is often regarded as the greatest champion that never was because he was always in the shadow of *Big Red*. In fact, Sham broke a track record and *still* lost. These two horses had a special power within them. While reading about this, it hit me: Secretariat's greatness started with the size of his *heart*.

That, my friends, is where it starts for us as well.

Physically, the heart controls the rest of the body; it is the engine that everything else runs on. Metaphorically, our hearts, or our souls, are the engine that fuels our lives. This is where gratitude *has* to begin. Now, I would argue that you could—and should—act grateful despite how you feel, but true gratitude occurs when your heart has undergone a transformation, when you no longer see yourself as a victim *of* your circumstances, but a victor *over* them. It could take years of acting grateful toward a certain situation for it to shape your heart, but it can happen. When true gratitude starts to sink in, it becomes a heart level change. We discover a new set of eyes; the eyes of our hearts.

A Quick Story on Perspective

When Liz and I set out to start our family, becoming pregnant was our last concern. We thought about names and the nursery, but never about actually becoming pregnant. We saw friends around us conceiving every day, and there was never a doubt that we would be parents. It took a nearly three-year battle with infertility before we had our first son, Matthew Jr. Shortly after our adventure into parenthood began, we received a once-in-a-lifetime opportunity.

I had just qualified for an incentive trip with my company for a week in Maui, Hawaii. So, with our eight-month-old at home with his grandparents, Liz and I flew to Maui for seven days. We had a blast while we were there, including some lifetime experiences that we will forever cherish. I must admit, though, that we didn't know how much that trip would change our lives. When we returned, we realized we had some extra luggage, and I'm not referring to Samsonite.

A couple of weeks after we returned home, I slowly awoke to the classic, walk-out-of-the-bathroom-holding-the-pregnancy-test wake-up call.

"Um, babe...I'm pregnant."

"Huh?" I wiped my eyes and came to my senses.

"Both tests were positive."

"Is this a belated April Fool's joke?"

"No, I'm serious."

As we set up an immediate doctor's appointment, my mind was racing. *How are we going to handle another baby?* These kids would practically be Irish twins.

Even as excited as she was, Liz was nervous too, and as we walked into the doctor's office, she said, "Remind me that God has a plan."

She was lying on the table waiting for the doctor when in walked a Jedi-looking, wand-yielding, white coat to perform an ultrasound. I begin to wonder *What plan? We're going to have two kids nearly fifteen months apart!*

The doctor interrupted my train of thought.

"Well, Liz, you're definitely pregnant, and your levels are incredibly high. You see, there's the heartbeat."

We were both staring at the static on the black and white screen, watching a faint flutter as the contrasting colors moved in sync.

"Well, that's interesting," our doctor observed. "There are two heartbeats!"

My mind moved so fast that I outran my mouth. "My kid has two hearts?"

The doctor laughed and replied, "You're having twins!"

I had to sit down on a bedside chair. There were flashes of panic amid the joy that we both felt. As I held tightly to Liz's hand, I glanced up to see her eyes welling up with tears. *Is this real life?* We both thought, *Maui, wowie!*

Our emotions were all over the board as we sought perspective. Walking in to the appointment, we didn't know how we were going to handle another baby, much less two. I recalled Liz's words, *Remind me; God has a plan.* As much as I wanted to believe that, I still followed up with, *What kind of plan is this?*

On November 28, 2011, we were blessed with two beautiful, identical twin boys: Wyatt Douglas and Greyson Boyd. They arrived about five weeks premature and as soon as they came into the world, they were swept away to the Neonatal Intensive Care Unit. As is common with premature boys, their lungs were underdeveloped, and they required assistance as they learned how to breathe. Seeing my boys hooked up to countless machines and cords quickly helped me gain the perspective I needed. Gratitude was easy to understand in these moments.

I was grateful for my boys and grateful for their doctors and nurses.

As they grew, I was astounded by their progress. We were able to bring them home just before Christmas on December 23, 2011. As most preemies do, they came home wearing heart rate/apnea monitors. These devices would accompany them for their first three months at home.

As their lungs continued to develop, the risk was that they could stop breathing, causing a *brady*, or *bradycardic* episode. This is where the heartbeat slows to dangerous levels, reducing oxygen to the brain. It was intense stuff to us, so we were grateful for the sensor pads across their chests. The machines would let out a high-pitched screech whenever their heart rates or breathing dropped below a certain, preset level. However, the devices also made the same sound if a sensor came loose. Imagine how many times, day and night, we went racing across the house, not knowing what triggered the siren.

Fast-forward twelve months. As the twins turned one, they were starting to become mobile and managed to contract every virus that came around. As it turns out, once a virus enters a house with three small children, it becomes a seemingly endless cycle of sickness.

On my birthday, my wife and I were ready for a much needed reprieve. We had plans to go to dinner and enjoy a few hours of each other's company. This quiet dinner was instead replaced by a trip to the emergency room. As much as I hate to admit it, I was angry. The soil of my soul was not ready for gratitude to take root. My soul had grown hard with bitterness and frustration.

It's amazing how easily it happens. That's the problem with negativity and ingratitude. It is always on the lookout, and once we give it a foothold, it jumps right back in where it left off, ready to wreck our perspective. Like a lion, creeping in the underbrush, waiting to attack.

> **Perspective**: noun [3]
> 1. the state of one's ideas, the facts known to one, etc., in having a meaningful interrelationship;
> 2. a mental view or prospect.

That night, as we headed back to the hospital, I was given a gift, an opportunity to refocus. As I parked my car and headed to my son's hospital room, I walked past the Neonatal Intensive Care Unit again. I thought about the families and doctors in there fighting for beautiful little lives. I thought about multiple friends who had lost their children. I thought about the countless stories of people facing tragic circumstances, yet remaining faithful and positive through them.

A sudden rush came over me. *Who was I to be bitter? Who was I to be ungrateful?*

It was that moment that caused me to begin understanding true gratitude and perspective. When I got to my son's room and saw him reattached to a breathing apparatus, yet still holding a sweet smile on his little face, the guilt from my own selfishness became real. I finally got it.

Gratitude is a simple choice regarding my circumstances, as painful as they might seem. Honestly, most of the time the situation is frivolous, yet I make it out to be so much more. Bitterness and selfishness exaggerate small issues into life-altering challenges. Perspective is a catalyst for real life change; transformation happens when we begin to renew our mind. A simple pivot in our thinking is all that it takes. It allows our hearts to receive the gratitude they were meant to thrive on.

Embracing Trials

Our foundation of gratitude will be shaken when we encounter trials. Unfortunately, our lives are filled with tragedy. Pain and suffering are real. Despite every effort to believe or see otherwise, we cannot escape it. However, can we view what others would see as tragic and trying in a different light? Is there a way to walk through suffering that will, in fact, make us stronger?

Again, I go back to Viktor Frankl's *Man's Search for Meaning* as he describes the struggles of his fellow campmates during World War II.

"Such people forgot that often it is just such an exceptionally difficult external situation which gives man the opportunity to grow spiritually beyond himself. Instead of taking the camp's difficulties as a test of their inner strength, they did not take their life seriously and despised it as something of no consequence. They preferred to close their eyes and to live in the past. Life for such people became meaningless."[4]

Frankl's experiences remind me that we have a choice to make.

So, how do we choose gratitude in those moments? We change our perspective.

The Bible tells an incredible story of perseverance regardless of circumstance. James was the half-brother of Jesus. He had witnessed his beloved brother brutally murdered without cause, and he had seen his friends persecuted for their beliefs, even to the point of death. Still, he writes these words.

> *Consider it pure joy, my brothers, whenever you face trials of many kinds, because you know that the testing of your faith develops perseverance. Perseverance must finish its work so that you may be mature and complete not lacking anything. (James 1:1–4)*

As I read this verse, something took shape in my mind. I looked at this passage backward. I rewrote the verses in this order:

> *To be mature and complete, not lacking anything, you must persevere. Perseverance is developed when your faith is tested. Your faith is tested when you face trials of many kinds. So when you do, be joyful. Pure joy, the greatest joy, only happens through the greatest trials.*

Allow that to sink in for a moment. Can it be true that pure joy only happens through the greatest trials? I think so. And I'll add that true gratitude is only seen in the midst of struggle. The word *complete* relates to richness, and it comes through the process of understanding gratitude regardless of circumstances.

When reading *Consider it pure joy to face trials,* a tendency to discount it develops fairly quickly when the word *trial* grabs your attention. However, when in reading *To be mature and complete,* the result is energy and hope. We have to endure the trials in order to see the maturity.

Helen Keller said, "No doubt the reason is that character cannot be developed in ease and quiet. Only through experience of trial and suffering can the soul be strengthened, vision cleared, ambition inspired, and success achieved."[5] Remember, Helen Keller was born deaf and blind, yet despite her limitations, she became the first with her condition to earn a Bachelor of Arts degree. Additionally, she became an author, activist, and lecturer, leaving a legacy that stands as a testament to gratitude in spite of tragedy. She was given the Presidential Medal of Freedom by Lyndon B. Johnson in 1964, one of our nation's highest civilian honors, and her spirit lives on today.

Seeking Gratitude in Trials

I understand it is easy to get sidetracked when challenges appear. When we see the storm clouds developing and hear the rumble of thunder, we start to question. Moreover, when it's raining on our heads, the wind is howling, and that rumble of thunder has become a flash of lightning, it simply becomes survival. In those moments, I hear familiar words from a familiar voice. *This too shall pass.*

My grandmother, Eloise Ham, was a wonderful woman, full of life and energy. She exemplified what the writer of Proverbs described as the wife of noble character. No one who knew her would say that she was anything short of amazing. Her 5'1" frame could fool you, but she traversed the Big Apple for her eightieth birthday and cut her own grass until she was eighty-three. She even fought off a carjacker at gunpoint in the mall parking lot at eighty-two years old. It was a fake gun under a coat, but she didn't know that at the time and proclaimed, "Show it to me," to her assailant.

She was one of fourteen children in her family and grew up on a farm in rural Timmonsville, South Carolina. She lived through the Great Depression, World War II, and was part of what Tom Brokaw referred to as *the greatest generation*. She truly earned that title.

One of her favorite sayings was, "This too shall pass." She always spoke it with such calm and ease that amazed me while I was growing up. For her, it wasn't a slogan; it wasn't lip service. She knew it to be true and believed it with every part of her heart.

We lost Grandma Ham in May of 2012 to cancer. She died one of the most dignified deaths I have ever seen. I was astonished by how she stared death in the eye and still smiled. She held such an inner peace. Never once did she fear the unknown. As she was dying, I sat next to her bedside, sobbing. She never shed a tear but simply reached down and grabbed my hand, saying, "It'll be just fine. This too shall pass."

I had the honor of speaking at her memorial. I spoke of her vibrancy and mentioned her favorite saying. She was able to embrace those words because her life exemplified living richly. As I look back, I see her staring at death with joy because she was complete in knowing *you make my life rich*.

Even now as I write, losing her is real all over again, but I choose to let it encourage joy in my heart because trials lead to perseverance, which leads to richness. I miss Grandma dearly, but I will always find joy in knowing *This too shall pass.* That reassurance is beautiful.

So, where are you with gratitude? Does your heart hold the "X-Factor"? An important thing to understand is that gratitude is only seen through actions. The size of your heart is found there as well. Quickly test your actions. What do you say and do in your life that reflects the gratitude you have in your heart? Or the opposite: what do you say and do that reflects the ingratitude in your heart?

Think of a few actions you've taken this week. Think of moments of recent struggle. How have you responded? I call this the heart test. You can tell yourself all day long that you have a grateful heart, but are you acting in accordance with it? Are you even thinking about how you're acting? If you're not seeing gratitude in your actions, you might just be saying, "I'm grateful." Remember, intentions are powerless. It is our action in conjunction with our intention that counts.

Expand Your Heart

If gratitude starts with our hearts, how can we seek to enlarge it? Much like seeking investment, this is an active process. The first step is understanding that gratitude cannot be mistaken for complacency. Being grateful doesn't mean, "I'm stuck here forever, and I have to be thankful for it." In fact, the opposite is true. What you'll find is that as you plant the seeds of gratitude, they will begin to grow and you will change. As gratitude takes root, allow the change, as uncomfortable as it may be.

Allow your heart to grow.

I love Dr. Seuss's *How the Grinch Stole Christmas,* particularly the end, when the Grinch's heart begins to swell. In the movie adaptation, Jim Carrey brought that character to life in such a way that he simply jumped right off the screen. In that defining scene when the Grinch hears the Whos singing carols despite not having any presents, he gets the picture of richness.

Maybe Christmas, he thought
Doesn't come from a store.
Maybe Christmas, perhaps
means a little bit more.

Like the Grinch, we've missed the point. When we see a true image of richness, it causes our hearts to swell inside of our chests. There's no denying the feeling.

What happened then,
Well in Whoville they say,
The Grinch's small heart
Grew three sizes that day.

During that scene, as Carrey brings the Grinch to life, he proclaims, "Help me! I'm feeling...I feel all tingly inside!" Gratitude wells up in his heart. As it happens, he doesn't ignore it or stop it. And we shouldn't either. [6]

I return to the analogy of the forest fire. After the fire, the forest doesn't stop growing. Life continues. The forest must embrace the richness of the soil, just as you must embrace the richness of gratitude in your heart. An awesome way to expand your heart is to practice gratitude. A simple way to practice is by recording it. Documenting gratitude creates a mental reminder that will stay with you once the experience has passed.

Whether you write it in a journal, take a picture, capture a video, create a voice recording, or simply jot it on a scrap of paper, start recording the things you are grateful for today.

I personally prefer writing, as it gives me incredible

clarity. When I define and put to paper what goes on between my ears, it grants me the ability to read beneath the surface. Find out which practice works best for you.

Additionally, the act of defining your struggles and, in turn, how you can respond is powerful as well. You will feel the polar opposites take shape in your mind. Choose the response that pursues gratitude, and it will push you toward richness. Can you think of five things you're thankful for? Ten? Fifty?

Make a list of things you're thankful for, or better yet, write a letter to a friend.

Letters from Dad is a great book by Greg Vaughn that encourages fathers to write letters to their families. It embraces the lost art of writing and encourages readers through writing personal, handwritten letters as a legacy for families. It's such an awesome concept that I plan to share with my boys when they get older. A few years ago, I received a letter from my own father, and I still reread it often, as it ignites gratitude in my heart. Simple acts like this help us to expand our hearts and allow gratitude to rise.

Stepping back into our previous principle, investing in others, we can make it a point to be grateful for others. This shows our appreciation for them and gives them incredible strength and energy.

A couple of my co-workers started a secret game they deemed the *Grateful Fairy*. Wanting to improve the morale of the office and welcome a couple of new team members, two co-workers started this practice of secretly leaving gifts and notes for fellow co-workers. During early morning and lunch hours, they would secretly thank fellow workers for various awesome acts. Sometimes, these acts would seem ordinary, like manning the desk for someone on vacation, or going the extra mile with a client, but their expression of gratitude made those mundane tasks awesome. Intrigued, I watched what was happening. First, everyone was consumed with figuring out who it was. It was like a real-life game of Clue. David left the chocolates for Joseph in the break room. People almost got mad, exclaiming, *I didn't do it!* refusing to accept responsibility for the grateful gesture. It was really hilarious to watch.

The two fairies were on top of it, even giving gifts to each other to keep everyone fooled. Pretty soon the accusations stopped and the awesome acts became more commonplace. People were more conscious of their actions and started consistently acting that way. Morale improved and productivity soared. That is the same year our office was recognized as the honor agency I mentioned previously. I'm not assuming it was directly related to holding doors or the "Grateful Fairy," but I don't find it coincidental. To this day, their identity is hidden and the "Grateful Fairy" still visits.

Gratitude Rising

Did you wake up this morning? I thought so. Find gratitude in simply rising each morning. I find this interesting: when you live a life focused on yourself, you tend to wake up based on your circumstances. For example, if you're going on a trip or have something fun planned, you pop right up, excited about all that is ahead. Heck, you might not even need coffee. You're so dang excited because the waking up is all about you.

On the flip-side, if it's another weekday, your rising is less motivated: *Don't look at me, speak to me, or come near me because I will destroy you.*

The only difference is what you think about the

circumstances you're waking up to. It's not the circumstances themselves; it's what you *think* about them. Simply shift your thinking and focus on the blessing of having another day. Rejoice in your many blessings as a way of allowing gratitude to rise inside of you.

On the Topic of Joy

So why bother with gratitude at all? At the root of gratitude is a three-letter word that seems very allusive, but something we long for—joy. Joy is a feeling of great happiness but can often be misplaced and that is why joy and gratitude are not to be confused as one and the same. It's interesting that gratitude will never fail to lead you to joy, but you can experience misplaced joy without gratitude. When this happens, we become over emotionalized as our surface-level joy is fleeting. I can't think of a better example than the holiday shopping season.

The day after Thanksgiving—commonly known as Black Friday—has always baffled me. People voluntarily sleep on cold street curbs and fight each other to save $300 on a television. Naturally, chaos ensues. There have been nationally reported incidents of shoppers breaking into fist fights over merchandise.

It puzzles me as to why people go to these great lengths for stuff, becoming highly emotional in the process. It's curious that we would spend hours waiting for the latest electronic fashion, yet fail to spend thirty minutes seeking gratitude and joy within their own lives. Then it hit me. Maybe they are searching for joy, which is why they become so offended when something stands in their way. Could that be possible? Is joy really saving $300 on a TV? It certainly can be, but that's not the source of the joy. It is much bigger than that. Saving $300 when you spend $1,000 that you don't have isn't joyful.

These individuals believe the savings, the TV, the stuff will fill a void with joy. I know I've been there and learned the hard way that it can't. It *won't*. That type of joy finds satisfaction in circumstance and in the event itself. That type of joy is fleeting. It's not even real joy, because it develops on the surface and stays there. Once the circumstance is over, it escapes us, only to leave us trying to duplicate it or recreate it at all costs.

The joy that we seek comes from the source. It comes from deep within us as a by-product of our gratitude. Everyone wants joy. We all seek life. The problem is, our ships are off course. The beauty of gratitude is that it leads to joy, and we get to choose! It's that simple and that available.

Chinese Philosopher Lao Tzu said, "The journey of a thousand miles begins with a single step."[7] Many understand this quote to say, "Regardless of how long the journey, you have to begin." Still, others will interpret, "The largest tasks can be broken down into single steps." As I pondered it myself, I placed it in the context of living richly and choosing gratitude. I thought, *On our daily journey to living richly, the first step is as important as the last.* Richness begins every day within our simple decisions and habits. You will either choose to live today richly, or you will choose to live today poorly. That thought process led to me creating a morning routine with my boys to help us remember.

I want my boys to greet each day with hope, optimism, and opportunity. I want them to believe that every day can be a great day. So, before I leave the boys each morning, I get down on one knee in front them and ask, "What are we going to do today?"

> **Joy**: noun [8]
> 1. a feeling of great happiness
> 2. a source or cause of great happiness
> 3. something or someone that gives joy to someone

The boys joyfully respond with excitement, "I'm going to have a great day!" Well, the twin say it more like, "Gate Dee," but they've got it. We exchange high fives, fist bumps, and kisses as I go on my way.

This may seem like a simple and unnecessary habit, but the other day, I learned it was so much more. I had to leave early that morning before the rest of the house was up and I didn't have a chance to go through our routine. When I returned home later that day, my oldest, MJ, came running to me. When I picked him up to wrap him with a hug, he pulled his head away from my shoulder and said, "I had a great day, Daddy!" I was joyfully reminded: *The journey of a thousand miles begins with a single step.*

When you start learning to hold on to gratitude in your life, you begin to anticipate greatness. You begin to see with a lens that you weren't previously aware of. In all honesty, you start seeing a bigger picture. Life becomes a beautifully interconnected story. That's the definition of My One Word, GREATFULL. It helps me clearly see my goal and place my gratitude in the context of my vision of richness. As we begin to see a bigger picture, the eyes of our heart are opened.

CHAPTER 9

Principle 4—Humble Yourself with Confidence

The Greg Sidden Story:
Becoming an Ironman

The fluorescent lights hum overhead. Their dull buzz increases the vague fog, creating a sense of dreaming. Has he been here for two minutes, two hours, or two days? He doesn't understand the furious work going on around him.

The work to save his life.

Now on his back, he can make out a number of men standing around him. They speak English, but use language he does not understand. They read charts and look at monitors, giving commands, "The patient is critical. His blood pressure is dropping from the internal lacerations."

In urgency, one of them yells, "Get him in the OR! Stat!" The confusion causes him to wince out a cry for help. A question that shows his concern and longing for clarity.

"Am I going to be okay?"

Dr. Lee, his attending ER physician, stares down at him. His reply is anything but comforting.

"I'm not sure."

In fleeting snapshots throughout his life, he gave consideration to what his final moments here on earth would look like. Would he want to cry? Would he be afraid? In this moment, he is neither. He thinks of his wife and his daughters. He longs to hold them. To touch them and tell them so many things.

Yet, in the midst of this chaotic scene, he feels an odd sense of peace. Deep within him, he feels a presence, a communion with a purpose greater than his own. It creates a calmness he can't explain. In this moment, he utters a prayer. "God. I know I'm hurt pretty bad, but I am at peace with You. Please be with my girls."

That is all he remembers.

On April 22, 2011, Greg Sidden was taking a very normal bike ride down a country round in rural Yadkin County, just outside Winston-Salem, North Carolina. Greg was a phenomenal athlete and in the best shape of his life. He placed great pride in physical activity and exercise, and was currently training for an Ironman, an endurance race in which athletes complete a 2.4-mile swim, a 112-mile bike ride, and a full marathon, 26.2 miles. The event takes competitors on a grueling 140.6-mile adventure, which, on average, takes nearly thirteen hours to complete.

His training and his life were very structured. His routine gave him the confidence he needed to perform. This particular morning, Greg was riding alone. His thoughts were his only company. He thought of his wife and his two daughters. His faith in God, something he had embraced since the age of ten. He thought about his career as an agency manager with North Carolina Farm Bureau Insurance Company. He thought about his upcoming race and pushing through the finish line.

His thoughts were suddenly interrupted.

A white Chevrolet Impala turned short from the oncoming lane, cutting in front of Greg. As he braced for impact, his body stiffened, and he threw his arms up to protect his face. He had little, if any, time to react before he violently collided with the right-front quarter panel of the vehicle. His body was launched from his bicycle and thrust headfirst into the windshield. At impact, he ricocheted off the car and came to rest, lifeless, in a nearby ditch. Greg remembers nothing of the accident, but would later learn that the impact from the wreck would leave the Impala totaled.

The human body is a miracle at work. More importantly, the physical trauma it can withstand is astounding. Greg's left side was completely crushed. He broke every rib and shattered both arms. However, the life-threatening damage was internal: a punctured lung, lacerated spleen, liver, and kidney.

For seven days, he lay in critical condition at Baptist Hospital in Winston-Salem. His attending physicians met with his family to impart the gravity of the situation. At any moment, his body could likely shut down.

Fortunately, it did not.

In time, the body will heal.

Greg taught me it is the mind and the soul where real healing occurs. Less than one year after his crash, Greg was racing again. In October 2013, just over two years after his accident, Greg would finish the Ironman he set out to complete back in 2011.

It started with simple walks in the park, as he was only able to travel steps at a time. It began with five-minute bike rides, pushing through the pain in his lungs as they became used to performing at such high levels again. Greg continued on.

Since his accident, Greg has completed four half-Ironman races, three marathons, and the granddaddy of them all, an Ironman.

When we talked about his physical accomplishments, I asked him, "Why?"

"As I lay there recovering, all I could think about was the gift I had been given. I felt like God gave me a wake-up call. As much as I hated to admit it, I wasn't in control. Honestly, that realization has given me the greatest confidence you can imagine."[9:1]

In a moment's time, Greg went from being in the best shape of his life to nearly losing it. In an odd way, humility has a way of finding you. When it does, it is your response that counts.

The virtuous conditions of humility and confidence seem to be independent of one another. Placed on the opposite sides of the scale, the more you have of one, the less you have of the other.

However, Greg has proven differently.

It is in humility where we find our greatest confidence. To walk in that confidence reflects great humility. Greg understands that his confidence is not his own. God's purpose in his life, God's gift of life, has given him new eyes.

Greg told me, "When everything is good, it's real easy to be positive. It's real easy to have faith then. The real test is how you respond to the fire. I had to understand that maybe I needed to be tested a bit."

Seeing how quickly it could all change, how quickly it could all be lost, gave Greg deep appreciation. He now lives with renewed purpose and efficiency, making the most of every day.

Actually, it was tragic news that helped Greg gain better understanding. A few months after his collision, Greg learned that around the same time of his accident, a father and his son lost their lives in a tragic cycling accident in Wilmington, North Carolina. David Doolittle and Trey Doolittle were hit head-on by a drunk driver early that same morning. At ages forty-six and seventeen, neither of them survived.

Greg doesn't purpose to understand the reasons why he was spared. He doesn't let the questions cripple him. He embraces his reality and continues, even taking part in a fundraiser put together in honor of the Doolittles for cycling safety and awareness.

"I refused to let this disable me, physically or mentally. I couldn't stand the thought of getting hooked on pain medications as a way to cope. I didn't want my girls to be afraid of any bad thing that could happen in life. I wanted to be an example to them in my faith, an example to everyone. God calls us to carry on."

Although I wasn't there, I have this image of Greg crossing the finish line last fall as he completed his Ironman in just under twelve hours.

I feel my emotion well up inside of me as I see this man embracing his gift of life, resting in the confidence that God would have him to continue.

Greg's story reminds us:

To live richly means to embrace the confidence we have in our high calling. The purpose to which we were destined. To walk humbly before our God.

Humble Yourself with Confidence

The phrase almost sounds like a contradiction: Humble yourself with confidence. How could you be confident and humble at the same time? The world would tell you that you can't have both, as it pits them in competition with one another.

By now, I think you understand that my approach is everything but conventional. In order to live differently, we must think differently. Therefore, it would only make sense to include a principle that seems contradictory. However, there is a special blend of confidence and humility that is required to obtain the richness we desire.

The fourth principle to living richly is:

H: *Humble yourself with confidence*

Our society, our culture, has little room for humility. In a world where everyone is out to make their name and stake their claim, pride in oneself is not only commonplace, it appears necessary. Boxing great Muhammad Ali summed up this mind-set when he said, "It's hard to be humble when you're as great as I am."[1]

When you define humble as an adjective, you get *not proud or arrogant, modest; courteously respectful.* With this definition, humility is seen as a condition. One could not possibly be humble and confident. However, if you define humble as a verb, you see to *lower in condition,* to make meek. This definition is active; an ongoing process. That is where we need to rest.

> **Humility**: noun [2]
>
> 1. the quality or condition of being humble; modest opinion or estimate of one's own importance, rank, etc.; courteously respectful; not proud or arrogant:

Confidence, on the other hand, is defined as *full trust; belief in the power of; assurance.* The way I see this principle is essentially placing yourself underneath the assurance that you're part of the story. You're not *the* story, but you are a part of it. You matter a great deal; if your part of the story is left out, part of the page remains blank. However, don't fall into the trap that the book is only about you. This is the formula to humbling ourselves with confidence.

When we look at popular culture around us, we see the opposite running wild. Athletes, celebrities, political figures all display blatant overconfidence. In fact, it has become the staple for creating our own personal kingdoms. The more overconfident and outlandish, the more destined we are for success. However, that type of success, popularized as the common definition of rich, is fleeting. That line of thinking has a shelf life, and then it spoils. We've all seen worlds come crashing down in a painful display of reality. Fly-by-night reality stars, one-hit wonders, and lottery winners bring life to rocker Jon Bon Jovi's song "Blaze of Glory".

The great basketball and life coach, John Wooden, said, "Talent is God-given. Be humble. Fame is man-given. Be grateful. Conceit is self-given. Be careful."[3]

We must learn how to walk the line between confidence and humility, as it will teach us how to respond today and give us hope in tomorrow.

The Ocean Speaks

Have you ever slept within earshot of the ocean? As you lie there, you become enveloped in the indescribable sound. At the very same time, the great water mass boasts both a low roar and a gentle whisper, as if pointing to something greater than itself.

Living at the coast, I've seen the ocean's ferocity during a storm that's unmistakably beyond comprehension. I've also seen the ocean calmly invite me to rest on its shores. The same ocean that holds the power seen in *The Perfect Storm* is the same ocean that advertisers use to lure you to the Caribbean. Like humility and confidence, seemingly opposite, they come from the same source.

As each wave comes crashing down, the ocean echoes something. Whether it be the vast ocean that lies beyond the shore or the hand of the Maker that sets it into being, the ocean resonates humility with confidence.

The gentle rumble of the ocean speaks of richness.

When you seek to live richly, carry confidence in something greater than yourself. It gives you hope that you are part of something bigger. You carry great power because you were created to matter. Henry David Thoreau said, "Men were born to succeed, not fail."[4] Don't believe so? Just look at how many lives will impact your day today. Look at how many people will cross your path and enable you to carry out your life. Think about the many who have gone before you and their impact. Ralph Waldo Emerson mirrored this idea when he said, "You are born to victory."[5]

However, when you fail, when you hurt, when tragedy befalls, you understand that there is a greater purpose than what is within sight. As the ocean exudes great power, remember, it is contained by its Maker. Somewhere within, I began to see this truth as well.

My pastor and friend has encouraged me with a prayer I cling to every day.

God, humble me by your presence, so that I don't have to be humbled by my circumstances.

The weight of that statement rests heavily upon my heart. The truth is, humility will come. Humility has a way of finding you. My encouragement to you is that you find it first. We must acknowledge our calling to humility to avoid being humbled. Find confidence in that you have a chance today to impact someone around you. You have the unique opportunity to make a difference. The question becomes, *What kind of difference will that be?* Be humbled by that opportunity.

Finding Humility

When is the last time you enjoyed the beauty of a sunrise?
The tranquility of a sunset?
The gentle power of the ocean?
The world around you exudes a greatness that is well beyond your control. It has always interested me that man has sought to explain the unexplainable rather than simply being humbled in its presence. I am certainly for progress and understand questions are essential. However, sometimes, when faced with something that blows us away, we should just rest humbly in the moment. I don't think it is possible for man to experience these moments without feeling a sense of humility. Without questioning that we are part of something bigger than ourselves. Whenever I watch the sun rise and set,

a radiant beauty sings a song to my soul. I am immediately humbled as I watch the horizon illuminate with the rising sun. Or, in the evening, I'm in awe as the late afternoon clouds turn colors I couldn't describe in my dreams. Oftentimes, I will stop the car and rest in that moment, basking in its richness.

To me, the sunrise gives me hope that another day is here. It reminds me that my story is not over; I have chapters left to write. It gives me confidence that I'm here to continue. For many years, I overlooked this simple blessing. It wasn't until I changed my perspective that I received the confidence I now write about. The trouble is, we fail to recognize; we fail to see. We get so busy with life's demands, we forget why we're even doing them in the first place. In this regard, we must intentionally create moments in our lives that allow us to humbly appreciate the glory of something greater than ourselves.

I recently traveled to Lake Tahoe. Split between the states of Nevada and California, it is the deepest freshwater lake in the US. The mountains seem to rise from the earth as towers of white-capped brilliance and at their base lies the crystal-clear water of the lake. You can't help but be drawn to its pristine beauty.

One day, we went kayaking out on the lake. Starting from shore, we made our way out into the deep, translucent water. As we did, the hum of the passing cars began to fade and the world around us became incredibly still. It was a silence that was full of sound. As I sat there on top of the water, looking at the mountain surround, I was humbled by how small I was. Nothing but a speck sitting in this vast wilderness. At the same time, there I was, out in the middle of the lake, confidently taking in my surroundings. My efforts to paddle into the setting put me in the middle of the story. I was part of the picture.

The truth is, you are a part of the story too. You are a part of that glory. If you weren't, then why are you here?

Reflecting Light

My boys love the book *Goodnight Moon* by Margaret Wise Brown. I can recite it from memory after three years of reading it every night. Have you ever heard of a *supermoon?* One out of every fourteen full moons comes closer to earth than before. In June of 2013, that cycle came around. During this perigee, as it is called, the moon is thirty thousand miles closer than at other times of the year. The result is a beautiful, bright moon that appears up to 15 percent larger and 30 percent brighter. I stared at the full moon during perigee and had this thought: *We only see the moon because it is reflecting light from the sun.*

Similarly, in our lives, we have the opportunity to reflect the light in us. The moon itself is beautiful, but it is only so because of the glory of the sun. The beauty of the moon is only seen because of the greater light the sun radiates, yet the moon benefits as well with the opportunity to be beautiful. If the moon were not in the presence of the sun, we would not see its light because it is only a reflection. Likewise, our life is a reflection of light. In your life, you are given the opportunity to be beautiful and great, simply by reflecting a greater light of richness within. Yet we must be reminded to humble ourselves with confidence. By practicing the principles we've discussed, we get the opportunity to radiate richness. What great confidence we can have as we begin to see our role in the story.

Creating Consistent Reminders

Our lives are full of traditions and habits. The word *habit* often denotes a negative connotation, doesn't it? Rather than swim upstream like salmon, we go with the flow; we take the easy road. Our habits become common, inconsistent with our dreams, and our rivers lead us into an ocean of average. If we desire richness, our habits must remind us of that desire and lead us to it.

Tom Morris is considered a public philosopher. In his fifteen years as a philosophy professor at Notre Dame, he brought philosophy to the classroom in a way that encouraged its pursuit. However, he felt a calling to take the message outside of the classroom and bring it into the public sphere.

In his book *True Success,* he unpacks the *7 Cs of Success* from principles handed down through the ancient philosophy greats such as Plato, Aristotle, Seneca, and many more.

His second C is a strong *confidence* that we can attain our goal. The ancient greats have taught us that confidence is essential. Tom quotes William James, who coined the phrase *precursive faith: Faith that runs ahead of the evidence.* Tom puts it this way:

> "We need confidence. And we can't wait for the evidence. We need to take matters into our own hands."[6]

However, it is Tom's fourth C that I think gives us some additional perspective. The fourth *C of Success* is a stubborn *consistency* in pursuing our vision. Once we've created a vision and have confidence, we must make sure that our actions are consistent with our goals. Tom writes:

> "One of the single most widespread and powerful

sources of failure nowadays is a form of self-sabotage. Self-destructive behavior. Thought and action inconsistent with the overarching goals and purposes people have."[7]

Isn't this so terribly true? If left unabated, our desire to walk the line between humility and confidence slides in one of two directions. We fall into the vice of either virtue. On one hand we are too humble; our meekness causes us to believe that we don't matter. Therefore, we don't take action and we fail to live richly. On the other hand, our overconfidence tells us that we are the story and we fail to have any impact because it is forced. Nothing turns people away faster than arrogance. Therefore, we must create habits that consistently remind us of our goals. Habits that cause us to remember.

Confidence: noun[8]

1. full trust; belief in the powers, trustworthiness, or reliability of a person or thing;

2. belief in oneself and one's powers or abilities; self-confidence; self-reliance; assurance;

3. certitude; assurance.

In pursuit of living richly, I've made it a point to redefine my habits and flip them on their heads. I've made a choice to swim upstream. I call it *Bowtie Friday*. For the past six years, I've carried on a Friday tradition of wearing a bowtie.

How did that begin, you ask?

It started with a dare.

When I began my career in insurance, I came to work my first Friday dressed for business. Someone hadn't let me in on the casual Friday concept. As everyone else casually enjoyed collared golf shirts, I was in a suit and tie.

Immediately, I thought it a novel idea to take a different approach. If everyone else was enjoying casual Friday, I would institute formal Friday. I'll admit, initially it was a fight-the-system mentality. Once I made my suggestion known, the barrage began:

"So what's formal Friday?"

Unsure myself, I quickly said, "I'll wear a bowtie!"

Laughter ensued.

"I dare you to wear a bowtie."

That was all I needed to hear. As they say, it was on!

One of the first days I wore the bowtie, I ran into a longtime family friend who quipped, "What's with the bowtie? You're not a bowtie guy, are you?" This puzzled *and* intrigued me at the same time.

What was this connotation that came with wearing a bowtie?

I can honestly say I still haven't figured it out and I may be the connotation. Either way, I made a decision then to embrace the challenge of changing that belief system. I wanted to redefine what it meant to wear a bowtie.

Could I create a habit that would remind me to live differently, to pursue confidence with a certain humility? While everyone else dressed in casual attire, could I swim upstream, don a bowtie, and at the same time, redefine the connotation?

I'm not suggesting that I have, but that has been my mission. Every Friday for six years, I've worn a bowtie as a simple reminder to live differently. I call it *Bowtie Friday*. As I began to think about this, I saw an eerie similarity.

In my writing, I am seeking something similar. While the world pursues its own definition of *rich*, one defined by financial wealth, can I turn that idea on its head? Can I redefine this paradigm?

That is exactly what we're doing. As we unravel what it means to live richly, I seek to redefine that word for you and for our culture. I seek to destroy the connotation that it carries and make it attainable for everyone, regardless of wealth.

I've heard it said that the decision to change happens at an instant, culture changes one person at a time.

I want us all to be confident that we can live richly. It then becomes about creating habits that remind us of our goal. Identify your habits and where they are leading you.

What habits are leading you in the direction of your aspirations? What habits are leading you away from them?

Once you make a choice, take steps in the direction consistent with your goals. Remember, the decision to change happens in an instant, but the process is one step at a time. As you walk your road to a rich life, take heart and continue. It is a rough road that few have the will to travel. Keep walking; clarity is on the other side.

God cannot tempt to virtue as we do to vice. He wants us to learn to walk and must therefore take away His hand; and if only the will to walk is really there, He is pleased even with our stumbles.

—C. S. Lewis [9]

The above quote gives me incredible hope for all of us. In short, Lewis is saying that God doesn't tempt us toward good, toward a virtue. He doesn't work that way. He deeply desires us to simply walk with Him. So much so that He removes His hand, allowing us to walk on our own will. As long as our will to walk with Him is there, he consequently takes joy even as we stumble in His direction. As you stumble with your eyes open and your heart seeking humility with confidence, the outcome will be clarity. My own life is the proof.

Clear Eyes

I consulted my journal during this writing process. I'm not a person who journaled religiously; I might have written a page here or there as I sought something for my own gain, but journaling wasn't a common practice. However, I can tell you that from what I've learned, it will be from here on. This journal was a gift I received after high school graduation and thirteen years later, it still contained many empty pages. As I pored over my past in search of clarity, I stumbled upon something that brought me to my knees.

My road to fatherhood wasn't a smooth, well-paved path. It began as a trek through a dark, dense forest full of obstacles. It was a battle.

Liz and I tried to start our family for nearly three years. Those who have shared in the struggle know it is a monthly replay of a movie you don't want to watch. You hope the ending changes, but as the curtain draws and the movie comes to a close, it doesn't. Yet your desire and hope cause you to rewind and start over.

Our struggle with infertility led us to a place in our marriage that neither of us would have ever hoped for. I've thought for the longest time, this part of my story, *our* story, was far from the richness that I have come to know. However, I've learned that every intricate part of our stories is orchestrated to collectively bring us to where we are. The stumbles, the heartache, the pain are all part of our unique journey. Remember, humility has a way of finding you. Remain confident.

Sometimes as we walk our paths, we only see the obstacles and feel the pain. However, when we emerge and look back, we see that we've blazed a path through the forest that only *we* could have traveled. A hole in the dense woods that is cut in the shape of us. The a-ha moment is only found when we keep walking. It invokes great confidence to continue on.

I found two journal entries tucked away on pages I haven't read since I wrote them. They were on back-to-back pages, despite having been written two weeks apart, thus betraying my inconsistency. I hadn't written anything in between.

In October of 2009, I went to visit my brother who was living in Florida, interning at Disney. I found myself back in the same spot where I'd spent those memorable moments with my Aunt Trish. I didn't notice the interconnectedness then, but now I see it. At the time, my wife and I had yet to become pregnant and had recently hit rock bottom in our marriage. We were in counseling, trying to rebuild a foundation that had been rocked by selfishness and apathy. Our lives were far from the Christian upbringing we once held to, and we knew it. We had turned back to our faith, a cry for help in our desperate time. As I sat there in the hotel lobby during breakfast, I glanced over and noticed something.

October 25, 2009

This morning, I was reading John 21, Peter's reinstatement by Jesus. A huge affirmation that God has and is redeeming us. He's not concerned about where we've been; He's concerned about where we're going.

I sat down to breakfast this morning and noticed a small black boy sitting with a white man. I overheard the young boy call him dad. I recognized a love in that exchange that had escaped me until now.

The boy wasn't born of that father, but it didn't matter. Regardless of our situation with not being able to have a child, I need to lose my pride. God, please honor this as I press toward that goal.

At the time, I had abandoned the idea of adoption because my pride stood in the way. For years before, I had fought the idea in my head and made sure Liz knew I was against it. In those emotions, I saw my own imperfection. In that moment, watching the interaction between this father and son, I recognized my own need for humility. Something was beginning to happen inside me. A slow awakening. A new connection with God.

Two weeks later, after I had returned home, I wrote these words:

November 11, 2009

There is truth in scripture that radiates peace and I cannot allow myself to fall away.

We have been heavily involved in fertility treatments this week and we have seen progressive growth in one of Liz's eggs. I know now that God is in full control over the whole situation. He has brought us here. I am humbled by His presence and confident in His Spirit. It's amazing and so far out of my reach that I simply have to trust it. There is nothing I can do beyond trusting Him. Today I learned how small I really am, and it made me very thankful.

Through God's amazing grace, that egg is now my beautiful, three-year-old little boy, Matthew.

It's not the outcome of the road that makes me joyful, although I know the blessing of hugging my boys. It's the fact that in the midst of that journey, Someone was walking with me who brings me to my knees.

Faith: noun [10]

1. confidence or trust in a person or thing;

2. belief that is not based on proof;

3. belief in God or in the doctrines or teachings of religion.

In all honesty, I am an emotional wreck even writing this. I'm dumbfounded as I stare at my journal and see this picture unfold. Reading this over and over as if to try and deny the words I had written nearly four years ago, I couldn't escape them. I had written, *I am humbled by His presence, yet confident in His Spirit.* In the middle of that experience, there was an active battle going on for my soul. There were forces at work that brought me through every moment as if purposefully placing me in the midst of my own struggles. It was my responsibility to remain confident as I walked my road. During the storm I didn't have the clarity I needed, but in hindsight, it all makes sense. Friends, that same battle I fought still continues daily. Not just for me, but for all of us. Yet we have to walk the road.

Could this really be true? Could this entire story, from my Aunt Trish to Gary Weller to Pastor Jackson to Peyton Fontenot to Greg Sidden to my own struggles really be God speaking truth to me? Would He dare to have me, in the midst of my crazy, seemingly unqualified life, share this with you?

I'm not one to presume what God would do, but as I read, longing for an answer to this question, I started to unveil truth in scripture that began to shine a whole new light on this unfolding revelation.

God's story is richness.

Redefine the Meaning of Rich

Having grown up in the 1980s, I can't help but have an affinity for *Star Wars*. George Lucas's *Star Wars* trilogy and latter prequel trilogy changed popular culture and blockbuster films. It's not surprising that the film series ranks among the top grossing of all time. These films set up a great battle in our minds, good versus evil, light versus dark, that is incredibly consistent with the Christian faith. If you recall the first film, *A New Hope*, Obi-Wan Kenobi is the old, wise Jedi Master imparting wisdom to a Jedi apprentice, Luke Skywalker. Young Skywalker holds the hope for the galaxy, hope to bring balance to the Force and an end to the Dark Side.[11]

Oddly, this reminds me of the books of Timothy. As I read, I had an image of a master imparting wisdom to his apprentice. The books of First and Second Timothy are actual letters written in the first century by the Apostle Paul to his "true son in the faith," Timothy. However, as I read through them this week, I had a strange feeling that Paul was writing to me.

Paul encourages Timothy to be confident, despite his youth. As I looked at the footnotes, I read that Timothy was in his thirties when he received Paul's letter. At this time, I am thirty-two years old.

As I continued on through chapter five, I came to words

I knew I was supposed to read. Paul warns Timothy of a trap that leads to temptation and many "foolish and harmful desires." Verse ten explains it very clearly.

For the love of money is a root of all kinds of evil. Some people, eager for money, have wandered from the faith and pierced themselves with many griefs. (1 Timothy 5:10)

That was me. That is part of my story. Wandering from the faith only to be pierced with grief. Take note that Paul doesn't say that money is the root of all evil; he says that the *love of money* is. He doesn't stop there. As I continued reading, Paul urges Timothy to flee from this trap and fight the good fight of the faith. Then, I read the words I knew God has for us.

Command those who are rich in this present world not to be arrogant nor to put their hope in wealth, which is so uncertain, but to put their hope in God, who richly provides us with everything for our enjoyment. Command them to do good, to be rich in good deeds, and to be generous and willing to share . . . so that they may take hold of the life that is truly life. (1 Timothy 5:17–19)

I was speechless; I just took that moment in. Paul's statement met me in the passion of my heart: redefine the meaning of rich. Throughout the writing of this book, I was given story upon story of true richness. Some of these stories were my own, but many of them were not. But all of them are His story.

And they continue.

The Richness of the Gospel

The Apostle Paul spoke of the importance of redefining richness nearly two thousand years ago. I believe it is still incredibly important today. Why? It's Paul's last line from First Timothy that provides me with hope for you and me both. That we may take hold of the life that is truly life. I want to know life that is truly life. I hope the same for you.

As I continued to search scripture, I saw this passage from Hebrews 10:35–36,

> So do not throw away your confidence; it will be richly rewarded. You need to persevere so that when you have done the will of God you will receive what he has promised.

Has God promised richness? Is that the story He is telling? I continued. Paul, again, in Second Corinthians writes:

> For you know the grace of our Lord Jesus Christ that, though he was rich, yet for your sakes he became poor, that you through his poverty might become rich." (2 Corinthians 8:9)

I don't want to presume to tell you what to believe. However, I do think, as we seek richness, we must see that we are part of a greater story. Our lives are intertwined in such a unique way that leaves us unable to deny it, if only we take the time to consider it.

As I was writing this exact portion of the book, I received a text message from a family member confirming this truth. She knew that I was writing the book and with encouragement, she shared these words from the Apostle Paul to the church in Philippi:

And my God will meet all your needs according to his glorious riches in Christ Jesus. (Philippians 4:19)

Somewhere along the line between confidence and humility, I think we find Jesus, waiting for us.

In His greatest act, just before His death on the cross, Jesus displayed this principle so beautifully. As the disciples sat in the upper room, arguing about which one of them was the greatest, Jesus, who had been given all authority under heaven, bent down on His knee and began washing their feet. He grabbed their dirty, dusty feet with his soon-to-be-pierced hands, He dipped a cloth in a basin of water, and He cleansed them.

Humble yourself with confidence means that we're not defined by who we are or what we've done, but rather, by whose we are. We are confident in Him who created us. The Bible teaches that we were created in the image of God, and Jesus promised us His spirit. I'm not a theologian; I'm not a pastor; and I have no professional training; but I can't deny this truth on my journey to define what Aunt Trish's nurse was saying. I know that my Aunt Trish was a follower of Christ in that she was a Christian. In hindsight, her life reflected a light within. And it's the same light I've seen in Gary Weller, Pastor Jackson, Sarah Fontenot, Greg Sidden, my grandmother, and countless others.

There is a correlation between the light of richness and the light of faith. I fully believe that we were created to live rich lives abounding in desirable qualities. That journey sometimes appears unfamiliar and likely painful. Keep walking, even if you stumble.

There is too much at stake for you to stop now.

Part Three
What's at Stake?

CHAPTER 10

A Lifetime Legacy

The sun slowly rises, radiating its warm glow. Shadows cast a blanket on the dew-covered ground. The clouds awaken with illuminated glory. The world wakes up. But *she* has been awake for hours this particular morning, just like every morning for the past sixty years. Every day she witnesses the beautiful symphony of daybreak.

There's never a need for an alarm. After sixty years, 12:00 a.m. has become her routine. However, even at eighty-five, the routine doesn't seem as such because it is her life. It is her purpose and her calling; she loves what she does. To her, it is everything but routine.

After a 5:00 p.m. bedtime, she's up at midnight, starting her day with a five-mile ride on her stationary bike, something she's done "her entire married life." After getting ready, she climbs in her white Lincoln Town Car and heads to work under the moonlit sky.

Ida Jean Mayhew carries on a legacy started long ago by her husband, Roscoe Mayhew, known affectionately as RB. His portrait still hangs on the wall, and she's not ashamed to admit that, as she prepares their small restaurant every morning, she still talks to him.

"I still give him a salute when I come in, 'I'm here!' After fifty-six years of marriage, you can't help but think about someone every day; even if they're gone."

After four years of cooking in the navy, RB married Ida and started their first restaurant, Mayhew's Barbecue, in 1946 just outside of Kings Mountain, North Carolina. Shortly thereafter, Vernon Rudolph, the founder of Krispy Kreme and a good friend, approached RB with a business opportunity. Knowing that opportunity often looks like hard work, they took a chance. They went on to own the first official Krispy Kreme franchise in 1949, opening three franchises before they sold back to corporate in the mid-1970s.

In 1977, they bought a small, one-acre tract off of Market Street and opened the Goody Goody Omelet House.

"We just wanted to have a small place that the family could operate; small and simple," Mrs. Mayhew said as she formed the hamburger meat into small patties for the day's patrons. I stood watching her at work as I listened to her words. She perfectly measured each quarter-pound of beef as we talked, yet she kept her eyes in constant contact with mine. She knew exactly what she was doing.

Although she's extremely humble and hesitant to admit it, the Goody Goody is everything but small and simple.

Those who have had the pleasure of visiting know the orange roof of the Goody Goody is a staple in Wilmington, North Carolina. True to their motto, "Just Good Food," they offer Southern soul fare with a smile and a side of encouragement.

This is their legacy.

My first experience at the Goody was in a baby carrier over thirty years ago. It was a day I certainly don't remember, but Mrs. Mayhew does. As we continued to talk, she said, "I can still see you in that bassinet on the table." It was, is, and always will be a tradition. Since then, my countless visits have spanned four generations; my grandfather, my father, myself, and now, my boys.

As I sat in the familiar surroundings with my three-year-old, I thought, *Mrs. Mayhew's story is unique, a lost testimony to a generation that is soon to be gone and values that seem to be disappearing. Her story needs to be told; the Goody has something to say.*

Like a sacred shrine that only holds thirty-five at a time, the small brick building is a refuge for those seeking good food and good company. One patron quipped, "It's one of the only places I've ever been where I can go alone and not be alone." Its foundation goes beyond the bricks; it's one of hard work, unbending morals, and unshakable faith.

In a world where employees come and go for the next best opportunity, Mrs. Mayhew has managed to keep hers, some for well over twenty years. Dave, for example, started washing dishes at fourteen. He's forty-one now and manages the open grill as if it were an art form. Fred, who is nearing twenty-three years, takes care of the pancakes, waffles, toast, and biscuits.

I asked Mrs. Mayhew about her employees' loyalty:

"I'm good to those that are good to me."

The conversations that have graced those walls, I know, are only part of the story. The smell of the bacon on the grill adds to the ambiance that is created every time you walk through the door. As ticket orders fly across the counter, sliding down the metal ticket holder, the drone of open conversations and the sizzle of the burgers blend into one big story.

A story everyone wants to be a part of. The line outside the door proves it.

Legacy

Mrs. Mayhew's legacy is unique because it allows others to create their own. Her 2:00 a.m. commitment has allowed those who enter to enjoy the company and conversations the establishment brings. With a smile all her own, she invests in her customers and calls her regulars by name. "Whatchya'll like?" is her familiar call as she grabs her pencil and scratches orders on her slender, white notepad.

When I asked her why she keeps doing it at eighty-five years old, she replied,

"I just love people. Retire? What's that? My daddy always taught me the value of working for yourself. As long as I'm here, I'll be here."

When I asked her if she knew the impact the restaurant had on so many people, she simply responded, "I just want them to get good food." And when I asked her what it means to her, she answered firmly, "I wouldn't sell it."

"There isn't any amount of money in the world that you would give up for is there?" I already knew the answer.

"You can't put a price on something like this."

As soon as I heard those words come out of her small, weathered frame, I knew Mrs. Mayhew was telling me a story. She embodies everything this book is about. She exudes living richly.

It is her legacy.

You can't help but have a special bond with someone whose dedication is carried out so unconditionally. In the end, when richness is achieved, it seems effortless—a thing of beauty. I can't stand to think of the day when her sweet smile and perfectly permed hair won't greet me with the hug and kiss I've become so accustomed. However, I know it will, as I think about RB sitting in his chair, thanking me every time I stopped by. I love Mrs. Mayhew dearly, as if she were my own blood. I love the Goody Goody. They will forever be a part of my story.

> **Legacy**: noun, plural legacies. [10:1]
>
> 1. anything handed down from the past, as from an ancestor or predecessor.

What I've gleaned from the stories of these folks, and what I hope you understand as well, is that richness is contagious. It infects those around you. It touches the souls and hearts of people. The ultimate blessing in living richly is that *it's not about you*. On the surface, that may seem disappointing, but follow me here.

It never has been about you or me, despite our efforts to make it seem that way. Honestly, we're the ones who *get* to live richly and we're the ones who *are* blessed; but in the end, if we make these choices, we transcend ourselves. We become part of the bigger story, because nothing great is ever focused solely on itself.

Living richly provides you and me the opportunity to leave a rich legacy, one that engages others in our story and encourages their own. It is people like Mrs. Mayhew who give me such a vivid image of what it means to live this way. She invests daily, chooses gratitude, and humbly serves her patrons with a confident smile. That's it. And you know what? Mrs. Mayhew will be remembered forever. Why? Because her story invites people in and allows them the space to create their own. Her legacy will continue for generations; that's just what a rich legacy does.

Living richly proves that you matter. You have a story and that story matters—to all of us. If this weren't true, then no one before us would have left their mark. We know richness when we see it; it speaks to our hearts. It calls to us in a familiar, unspoken voice that is undeniable. All too often, we shut it off and don't listen. We cripple ourselves with fear and false beliefs, and we lie defeated, thinking that we don't matter. Nothing could be further from the truth.

CHAPTER 11

A Rich Legacy Transcends Death

As I write about the Goody, I think fondly of my times there. The Goody was the setting for many of my lessons about richness, particularly from my grandfather. Every other Friday during high school, my Paw-Paw and I would share our corner booth. Alongside our eggs, grits, waffles, and coffee, we would enjoy rich conversation.

He was my rock.

I never knew my grandfather as a young man, laboring in the sun on a farm in rural South Carolina. His best friend was an African-American farmhand. Heads turned in the 1930s as the two of them walked alongside each other, watching them separate when they went into town for school or even a picture show.

I never knew the man who approached my grandmother while they were in school, asking her on a date, feeling the same nervousness we've all felt when our hearts beat through our chests as we approached to ask the question.

I never knew the man who served our country in Japan at the age of eighteen. The sorrow he felt leaving his family, the only life he ever knew.

I never knew the father who worked long hours to provide for his three sons. Pursuing opportunities through hard work and honesty would eventually lead him to Wilmington, North Carolina.

But I did know the man whose well-deserved retirement came at the age of seventy.

I knew the man whose cancer diagnosis arrived a year later.

I knew the man who remained optimistic, although he was hurting. The man who said to me, "When you finish your freshman year, I'll be done with my treatments."

That was not how his story would end. That time never came. Paw-Paw was tired of fighting. He was tired of hurting. One Sunday morning in June of 2001, he took his life in his own hands. I still feel the rawness, the questions, and the pain that followed.

This was the day my rock crumbled.

When we arrived at the hospital, we learned he was still alive, but on life support. My dad wanted me to go with him to my grandfather's hospital room. Confusion and fear filled my young, nineteen-year-old mind, but I stood by my father as he went to tell *his* father good-bye. The hallway to his room seemed like a never-ending pathway to a place I never wanted to go. As we entered his room, I saw my Paw-Paw, lying on his bed, his life sustained only by the breathing apparatus affixed to his mouth. I was frozen, experiencing the moment, paralyzed from speaking.

My father walked in front of me, slowly approaching his dad. As he dropped to his knees, I gently placed my hand on his shoulder. I could feel his anger and heartache through my fingertips as an emotional battle raged within him. Through questions and tears, I heard my dad say, "You were a great father."

The memory of that exchange is impressed on my soul, forever etched into my story.

Soon after, our pastor and friend, Tim Russell, came in to pray with us. He prayed for Paw-Paw, and a few minutes later, I watched my grandfather take his last breath. For years that memory has haunted me. Circumstances beyond my comprehension. Questions without answers. Only through time have I come to realize, sometimes there are no answers.

My belief in that statement doesn't make it any easier to write. I guess a better way of saying it is, in regard to some questions, it is not our purpose to have answers. It is our purpose to continue. In the midst of these moments we are defined. We are either frozen by their impact, or we press onward. We can let those moments derail us, or we can let them push us to carry on. Let us carry on. We must press into the greater calling in our lives and press into our faith, choosing our legacy.

These moments *will* define us. We get to decide how.

It's always been difficult for me to understand those circumstances, until now. I have come to realize that it is not my place to always understand. However, we don't need answers in order to take action and do what we know must be done. This is when we must lean into the principles of richness and live out the calling of our lives.

I see richness as a flame, burning bright within. I saw that flame in my Paw-Paw. Like honorary torch bearers, we have the opportunity to fan that flame or snuff it out. The flame of richness that is in each of our hearts has been passed down to us through a greater story, and it is up to us to keep that flame alive.

John Maxwell, the great business leader and author reminds us, "Your candle loses nothing when it lights another."

My grandfather and I had a little secret between us. As he saw me growing, he decided it was time to teach me. Only in looking back am I able to see the symbolism in our secret exchange. On occasion, in his handshake, he folded a twenty-dollar bill inside his palm. He would chuckle as I felt it pressed against his warm, weathered palm. It had little to do with the money; he was giving me a small taste of richness every step of the way. He was passing it on to me.

My grandfather's richness didn't die with him as I previously thought; his story lives in me, just as it was passed to my father before me. That is my motivation: to continue his rich legacy.

He was not afraid to admit his *brokenness*. He realized his mistakes and struggles made him stronger. I choose responsibility and forgiveness as I heal.

He loved and *invested* in his family and those around him. His life wasn't about himself. That honor is now mine. I will serve others and give of myself. I choose to love.

He believed in *gratitude*, always choosing to see the best in people and circumstances. I must live with a thankful heart as I seek the greatness inside of me. I choose to be grateful.

He *walked humbly with confidence.* He knew he was part of a bigger story. And I recognize that I matter, and my impact affects others' lives daily. I choose to embrace this challenge with humility.

CHAPTER 12

Live What You Write

S ome uncanny events have taken place during the writing of this book that I cannot leave out of its publication. In an odd way it's a clear reassurance, just like I experienced when I began writing these words. But now I now see that these events are simply part of the story I've been called to tell. They are a continued part of this journey to redefine a word: *rich*.

As I continued, I encountered a challenge I never expected: a diagnosis of my own.

"Matt, we knew the spot was atypical. The biopsy has shown that it is a spreading malignant melanoma."

"Does that mean it was cancer?"

I didn't need to hear her words to understand the answer

to my own question. The look in her eyes told me before her head began gently nodding.

"But, the good news is, we got it. It's gone. However, for preventative measures, I want you to go next week to have a larger area removed." Her partial smile was gentle and left no hint of fear. Her calmness and grace in delivering those very difficult words allowed me to keep it together as I gathered my things and processed the shocking news. Her sweet, kind hug was reassuring. I felt her own anxiety, the kind when a doctor is also a friend. She hurt for me; I could feel it. As if what I'd just heard wasn't enough, she looked me in the eyes and gave me a dose of perspective.

"I'm thankful for whatever angel brought you in here last month. In a year, we may have been having a much different conversation. God has your back; you're going to be fine."

As I walked down the hallway leaving the dermatologist's office, my mind began racing—every thought and emotion at war with each other. Fear, doubt, and anxiety were violently and aggressively attacking me from every angle.

Cancer? Me?

Malignant melanoma is a very aggressive form of skin cancer, usually associated with overexposure to the sun. In my case, sun exposure didn't appear to be the problem; I believe that's why my dermatologist and I were both so shocked. More so, that's why I was so afraid.

What if it has already spread? What if it comes back? What about my boys?

The hardest part was telling my wife, who lost her father at the age of forty-three to cancer. Equally as difficult was telling my own parents and younger brother. The lump in my throat seemed to block the words from coming out.

"She said it was cancer."

This disease has been rampant in our family and countless others. A wretched, unrelenting disease that we cannot seem to escape. From Aunt Trish to my grandmother, to both grandfathers, cancer has been the greatest cause of loss in my life. And now it was a page on my own medical chart. There's no such thing as just skin cancer when the diagnosis is your own.

However, I held on tight to the doctor's words, "God's got your back. You're going to be fine." Within that exchange, I felt a peace that I wasn't alone. In fact, I knew I wasn't. And this book was my reminder.

As I mentioned, I've engaged the process of My One Word for years now; this year was no different. As I pondered my choice for 2014, I kept feeling the word *trust* placed on my heart. Honestly, I thought it had to do with trusting God with the writing of a book. Now, standing in the midst of a cancer diagnosis, it held new meaning. It had to do with trusting God *with my very life*.

I wrote this book about my journey to redefine rich months ahead of my own struggle to live out the principles I had written. It felt like God had me write these words, if for no other purpose, for myself.

I immediately recalled the memories of my last times with my Aunt Trish. Her dignity as she faced her diagnosis took on new depth. She was rich, indeed. I remembered that fateful conversation between her and her nurse. And then, there were those words, the ones where this all began:

You make my life rich.

They contained life. They contained hope. I knew their deeper purpose; I trusted in them.

Finding Purpose

To prevent further spreading and for the purposes of additional testing, I was scheduled to have surgery to remove a total of four inches of tissue from my side, ensuring the cancer had not and would not spread. My surgeon was Dr. Greg E. Viehman.

Dr. Viehman is brilliant. He graduated first in his class from Jefferson Medical College and went on to complete graduate training at the University of Pennsylvania and Duke University Medical Center. One of the nation's leading dermatologic surgeons and lecturers, he's also an author.

But his book isn't about his medical knowledge. Although he's written numerous scientific research articles, his book is strikingly different. *The God Diagnosis: A Physician's Shocking Journey to Life After Death* has everything to do with his own story of faith.

As I walked into his waiting room the day of my surgery, I noticed a replica King James Version Bible from 1611 sitting on a lectern. It was comforting reminder of the Great Healer. In the midst of my surgical procedure, I felt God's presence; He was right there with me in every passing moment.

My surgery required only localized anesthesia, so I was awake throughout the entire procedure. This allowed me to talk with Dr. Viehman, so I did. Do you know what we spoke of?

Richness.

We talked about our faith, finances, personal, and professional lives working in connection with one another to radiate richness.

We talked about brokenness. Both our physical and spiritual condition. This foundation is where we begin.

Recognize you're broke[n]

We talked about others. Our calling to be a light as we invest in and seek the investment of those with whom we are entrusted.

Invest in others

We talked about gratitude and the importance of perspective. The gifts of breath and life. The gifts of love and laughter. It's our choice.

Choose gratitude

And lastly, we spoke of humility and confidence. How we must learn to enjoy each in equal parts. We are part of a bigger story, and our lives have purpose. We must humbly accept that call.

Humble yourself with confidence

For some, our cancer is physical, a disease that has the potential to ravage our bodies. At times, it can be slowed and even removed, but it doesn't rid us of our condition. My own scar reminds me that physically I have been pierced in order to be saved.

> **Purpose**: noun. *12:1*
> 1. the reason for which something exists or is done, made, used, etc.

That is a humbling thought.

However, there is a much deeper cancer. One that ravages our soul. My own experience has brought even more awareness of its existence. It is a spiritual cancer whose spreading cannot be stalled by our own efforts. The beauty is, there is One in whom we can place our trust because He was pierced so we could be saved.

He was pierced for our transgressions . . . by His wounds, we are healed. (Isaiah 53:5)

The Bible teaches us that by Jesus's wounds, ours have been healed. Our spiritual brokenness no longer holds power over us. Because our spiritual condition has been redeemed, our exterior, physical condition becomes secondary. The nails in His hands and feet and the piercings in His side provide redemption. And there's nothing we can do to earn this.

It is His grace, freely given, that gives us life. That is our richness.

Seeing this imagery unfold in the storybook of my life brings me peace, the same peace I hope for you.

God's story is rich.

Christ endured the poverty of a broken body and a broken spirit so that, in Him, we could have life. God is at work, even in our brokenness. That is where this journey began for me and that is what I come back to in the end.

My prayer is that the story wouldn't end here. Why? Because there are many more who don't realize that they're sick. I was met head-on with my physical sickness, and it provided a reflection of my own spiritual condition and the great cost to allow me freedom.

It is with absolute joy that I share the latest report. All of my cancer has been removed and the clear margins require no additional treatment. I know this is but one opportunity to embrace the richness that life has for me regardless of my exterior circumstances.

I believe you will have these opportunities as well.

My prayer is that you choose richness.

Awake My Soul

This book has not only changed my life, giving me new perspective on my past, it has reshaped the way I live. My hope is that, in some way, it has encouraged you as well.

This journey has been a blessing to me. As I've pondered into the words spoken to my aunt, *You make my life rich,* they have changed who I am and who I am becoming, forever.

I don't hope the same for you. I don't hope that you discover what it means to live richly because I know it's too important to miss.

I dare you to.

Mumford and Sons wrote a beautiful song called *Awake My Soul.* Music speaks to me, and this song stirred my thoughts.

As I listen to the lyrics, their origin comes to mind. The line "Awake my soul" was once penned by a young King David. In Psalm 57, the future king who has yet to be crowned is on the run from King Saul, who is out to kill him. David is hiding in a cave, fearing for his life. It is in that cave where David penned these words:

Have mercy on me, my God, have mercy on me,

for in you I take refuge.

I cry out to God Most High

He sends from heaven and saves me . . .

My heart . . . is steadfast, I will sing . . .

Awake, my soul!

David saw the cave was no place to live. His soul longed to be awakened.

I have come to realize that so many of us, including myself, have taken shelter in our caves from time to time. We're in hiding, fearful of the life we are called to live. We all invest in something, hoping an awakened soul would be the outcome. We are all seeking richness in one way or another. Yet, all too often, this pursuit leads us back into our proverbial cave. Seemingly, the awakened soul eludes us.

Until now.

Our souls long to awaken; they long to live richly because that is what they were created to do. Richness waits for you to step into its light. It only takes a step for you to move in that direction.

In Matthew 5:16 Jesus instructs,

You are the light of the world. Let your light shine before men so that they may see your good works and praise your Father in heaven.

In my search, I have discovered this truth. Living richly, at its core, is living for God. Having our souls awakened by His love and redeemed by His grace. A rich life is simply a reflection of His glory and peace while resting in His provision. He longs for us all to live richly.

From this abundance, we're called to flood that richness, that hope, into others.

This may be so incredibly far from the message you have heard regarding Christianity. In many ways, it has been for me. This journey has been enlightening and is one I will continue to learn about. But, from here, we must take action. We must begin our race.

In Hebrews 12:1, we are given this encouragement,

Let us run with perseverance the race marked out for us.

Life is full of moments that can define you, derail you, or drive you. You choose how you respond. The tragedy of difficult times is when we let them defeat us. You're not alone. Refuse to be defeated. Fight for richness. Run your race. Persevere.

Becoming rich isn't measured in numbers or years. It can't be qualified. As I've said, it's in your actions, which is the legacy you leave by the story your life tells.

I imagine there will come a day when words will be spoken of us upon our death. My challenge is that we live so that the words, *You make my life rich,* are etched on our gravestones. Remember, everyone has a story and that story matters in ways we cannot begin to understand. Your page is part of the story. Without you, the book is unfinished.

I'm leaving the last page blank; as our reminder that this story is not over; your story is not over.

You are here. Your story is waiting to be created. May it be a rich one.

Your Rich Life

I know well that stories of richness are inside of you, and my prayer is that this book has helped you gain a better understanding—a new perspective—of them. With that being said, I long to hear your story and to be enriched by your experiences, and I would encourage you to share with us as part of the Live Richly Challenge.

Please contact us online at www.mattham.com/contact to share your story, and we will let you know how you can be involved.

You can also share on social media using the hashtag
#RedefineRich

More from Matt Ham

For weekly perspectives to enrich your life, visit:
www.mattham.com
and sign up for the Live Richly Newsletter for
encouragement and updates on resources for
group or personal study.

Matt hosts a weekly podcast titled, Redefine Rich:
Subscribe via iTunes at www.mattham.com/itunes
or Stitcher Radio at www.mattham.com/stitcher.

To contact Matt for speaking engagements, please email
speaking@mattham.com or call (910) 619-4644.

More on Redefine Rich

For more on this book or for opportunities to
purchase additional copies, visit:
www.redefinerich.com.

Acknowledgments

I can't begin to express my deepest gratitude for everyone who has been such a partner in this journey. First, I must thank God, the Author and Giver of Life and the source of unending riches. Second, my wife, Liz. If it were not for your unending dedication to our family, your gracious understanding, and your anchoring encouragement, I would not have been able to write this book. To my boys, Matthew, Wyatt, and Greyson: your tender hearts and inquisitive minds have been so motivating during this process. I'm glad to say that "Is your book finished, Daddy?" is a phrase I can definitively answer with a resounding "Yes!" I pray that one day when you're able to read these words, they will sing of my deep love for each of you. To Mom and Dad: thank you for a picture of richness over the past thirty-two years and for being so willing to share your richness with those around you. To Doug and Susu: thank you for loving me as your own and for such a consistent presence of generosity throughout my life.

To Uncle Larry: thank you for allowing me to expose the vulnerability and the real heartache of losing such an amazing part of our lives. My sincerest hope is that this would carry on the legacy that Trish began and that countless lives would be enriched by her story.

A special thank-you to Gary and Cathy Weller, Pastor Jackson Mwangi, Port City Community Church, Sarah and Ron Fontenot, Greg and Kristy Sidden, and Mrs. Ida Jean Mayhew. I stand in awe of each of you and am extremely blessed that the Lord granted us the opportunity to meet. Moreover, for your grace in allowing me the privilege to tell your stories. You make my life rich.

I couldn't continue without mentioning my friend, Tom Morris. Tom, I have admired your wisdom and your success for many years, so to be able to glean from you these timeless truths has been an honor. Thank you for seeing something inside of me that needed to be drawn out and for seeing that process through. To Craig Wheeler: for your help in organizing my thoughts and for giving me specific direction. To Mike Ashcraft: for your continued affirmation and belief in what God is doing.

To Jim Van Eerden and your team at LIFE⁹ Books: thank you for the honor to partner with you to make this dream a reality. I am grateful for your belief in this movement to enrich the lives of many. To Anna Floit of The Peacock Quill: for your abilities as a wordsmith, thank you for your help in bringing this perspective to life. To Sarah Morris of Goodnight Gracie Photography: for the amazing images you've created; and to Sam Torode: for shaping them into the cover art that speaks so directly to the heart of this message. To Mike Loomis: for your knowledge and guidance during the final stages of turning this book into what it has become. To my friends at LaunchOut: your belief in my dream and your willingness to dream has been a driving force behind this book's completion. To Andy Andrews, Robert D. Smith, and the team: your encouragement to persist without exception was a rally cry from day one. Chris LoCurto: thank you for a coach's heart and for helping me tuck in my cape.

Finally, I have to thank Melanie Fogleman, my Aunt Trish's nurse. Since the writing of this book, I am so grateful that we have been able to connect. Your words have sent a ripple into eternity. They have and will affect the lives of many, giving us all the hope that our own words can do the same. Thank you for making our lives rich.

Notes

Foreword:
1. C. S. Lewis, An Experiment in Criticism (England: Cambridge University Press, 1961), 141.

Chapter 2:
1. For more information on Disney, see http://disney. com.

Chapter 3:
1. Tim McGraw, "Live Like You Were Dying" (United States: Curb Records, 2004).
2. It's a Wonderful Life, film, Frank Capra (1948: RKO Radio Pictures), medium.
3. Dictionary.com. "Rich." http://dictionary.reference. com/browse/rich?&path=/ (Accessed October 24, 2014).

Chapter 4:
1. Michael Jordan, I Can't Accept Not Trying: Michael Jordan on the Pursuit of Excellence (San Francisco, CA: Harper San Francisco, 1994), 129.
2. Dictionary.com. "Can." http://dictionary.reference. com/browse/can?s=t (Accessed October 24, 2014).
3. Dictionary.com. "Intentional." http://dictionary. reference.com/browse/intentional?s=t (Accessed October 24, 2014).

Chapter 6:
1. Garth Brooks, "The River" (United States: Liberty, 1992).

2. Dictionary.com. "Broken." http://dictionary.
   reference.com/browse/broken?s=t (Accessed
   October 24, 2014).

3. Anahad O'Conner, "The Claim: After Being
   Broken, Bones Can Become Even Stronger," New
   York Times, Oct. 18, 2010, New York edition.

4. For more information on the Dave Ramsey team
   and his books, see http://www.daveramsey.com/
   home/.

5. Adele Laurie Blue Adkins, "Rolling in the Deep"
   (London: Eastcote Studio, 2010).

6. For more information on The Lord of the Rings,
   see http://en.wikipedia.org/wiki/The_Lord_of_
   the_Rings.

7. For more information on Star Wars, see http://
   en.wikipedia.org/wiki/Star_Wars.

8. Viktor E. Frankl, Man's Search for Meaning
   (United States: Beacon Press, 1959), 87.

9. Dictionary.com. "Responsibility." http://dictionary.
   reference.com/browse/responsibility?s=t (Accessed
   October 24, 2014).

10. Andy Andrews, Mastering the Seven Decisions
    (United States: Thomas Nelson, 2008).

11. Dictionary.com. "Forgiveness." http://dictionary.
    reference.com/browse/forgiveness?s=t (Accessed
    October 24, 2014).

Chapter 7:

1. Dictionary.com. "Invest." http://dictionary.
   reference.com/browse/invest?s=t (Accessed October
   24, 2014).

2. Brainy Quote. "Ralph Waldo Emerson quote." Accessed October 25, 2014. http://www.brainyquote.com/quotes/quotes/r/ralphwaldo118171.html.

3. Investopedia. "Compound interest." Accessed October 24, 2014. http://www.investopedia.com/terms/c/compoundinterest.asp.

4. John Donne, Devotions upon Emergent Occasions (Kingdom of England: 1624), Meditation XVII.

5. Brainy Quote. "Maya Angelou quote." Accessed October 25, 2014. http://www.brainyquote.com/quotes/quotes/m/mayaangelo385317.html.

6. Brainy Quote. "Eleanor Roosevelt quote." Accessed October 25, 2014. http://www.brainyquote.com/quotes/quotes/e/eleanorroo393444.html.

7. Dictionary.com. "Generosity." http://dictionary.reference.com/browse/generosity (Accessed October 24, 2014).

8. Robert D. Smith, 20,000 Days and Counting: The Crash Course for Mastering Your Life Right Now (United States: Thomas Nelson, 2013), 44.

9. Dustin Wax, "Don't Be Eeyore," Lifehack. Accessed October 24, 2014. http://www.lifehack.org/articles/lifestyle/dont-be-eeyore.html.

10. Dr. Seuss, I Can Read with My Eyes Shut! (United States: Random House, 1978).

11. Brainy Quote. "Martin Luther King Jr. quote." Accessed October 25, 2014. http://www.brainyquote.com/quotes/quotes/m/martinluth137105.html.

Chapter 8:

1. Dictionary.com. "Gratitude." http://dictionary. reference.com/browse/gratitude?s=t (Accessed October 24, 2014).

2. Mike Ashcraft and Rachel Olsen, My One Word: Change Your Life with Just One Word (United States: Zondervan, 2012), 25.

3. Dictionary.com. "Perspective." http://dictionary. reference.com/browse/Perspective?s=t (Accessed October 24, 2014).

4. Viktor E. Frankl, Man's Search for Meaning (United States: Beacon Press, 1959) 93.

5. Helen Keller, Helen Keller's Journal: 1936–1937 (Garden City, NY: Doubleday, Doran & Company, Inc., 1938), 60.

6. Dr. Seuss, How the Grinch Stole Christmas (United States: Random House,1957).

7. Brainy Quote. "Lao Tzu quote." Accessed October 25, 2014. http://www.brainyquote.com/quotes/ quotes/l/laotzu137141.html.

8. Dictionary.com. "Joy." http://dictionary.reference. com/browse/Joy?s=t (Accessed October 24, 2014).

Chapter 9:

1. Brainy Quote. "Muhammad Ali quote." Accessed October 25, 2014. http://www.brainyquote.com/ quotes/quotes/m/muhammadal145924.html.

2. Dictionary.com. "Humility." http://dictionary. reference.com/browse/Humility?s=t (Accessed October 24, 2014).

3. John Wooden, They Call Me Coach (United States:

McGraw-Hill Professional, 2003).

4. Brainy Quote. "Henry David Thoreau quote." Accessed October 25, 2014. http://www.brainyquote.com/quotes/quotes/h/henrydavid131254.html.

5. Bartleby. "Ralph Waldo Emerson quote." Accessed October 25, 2014. http://www.bartleby.com/90/0810.html.

6. Tom Morris, True Success: a New Philosophy of Excellence. (United States: Berkley Trade, 1995).

7. Ibid.

8. Dictionary.com. "Confidence." http://dictionary.reference.com/browse/Confidence?s=t (Accessed October 24, 2014).

9. C. S. Lewis, Screwtape Letters (New York: HarperCollins, 2001), 39, 40.

10. Dictionary.com. "Faith." http://dictionary.reference.com/browse/faith?s=t (Accessed October 24, 2014).

11. For more information on Star Wars, see http://en.wikipedia.org/wiki/Star_Wars.

Chapter 10:

1. Dictionary.com. "Legacy." http://dictionary.reference.com/browse/Legacy?s=t (Accessed October 24, 2014).

Chapter 12:

1. Dictionary.com. "Purpose." http://dictionary.reference.com/browse/purpose?s=t (Accessed October 24, 2014).